Some Adventures Outdoors

(And In The Kitchen!)

A Lifetime of Adventures and Recipes

STAN YOCKEY

ISBN 979-8-9901403-4-9 (softcover)
ISBN 979-8-9901403-3-2 (hardcover)
ISBN 979-8-9901403-5-6 (ebook)

Printed in the United States of America.

To my parents Don and Kay, who introduced me to the outdoors, and to my wife Susan, who encouraged me to go on these adventures and patiently helped me develop the kitchen skills needed to create the menus in this book.

Contents

Preface

Since even before my earliest memories, I've loved the clear waters and scenic beauty of wild streams and rivers throughout the western United States as well as the sights and scents of soaring mountains, open croplands, and sagebrush-covered hillsides.

For example, at age one, while my parents fly fished the spring runoff of an eastern Colorado stream, I "swam with the fishes" by crawling into the water to be swept downstream and caught by the back of my diapers by another fisherman. Then, at age four, I slipped off an overhanging bank into the clear but frigid water of the Bogachiel River on Washington's Olympic Peninsula, requiring my father to "fish" me out of the pool by my ankle. Fortunately, I survived both experiences and have developed a healthy respect for the potential dangers, as well as the beauty, of all rivers.

As I grew up, hunting upland birds also became part of my upbringing, and I learned many life lessons from being outdoors when I was young: learning about many different kinds of wildlife and their habitats, seeing many different areas of the state of Washington, and meeting interesting people.

So if you love the outdoors—its beauty, bounty, and diversity—I am just like you. If you enjoy being creative in the kitchen as you prepare delicious and sometimes unusual meals for your friends and family, I am just like you. And if you take pride in savoring the rewards of our outdoor adventures in a carefully planned and prepared meal that makes the most of what you harvest in the field, I am just like you. I am not a professional fisherman, hunter, or chef—I am just like you.

This book is the product of an abiding love and appreciation for the outdoors, shaped by many unique experiences along the way; and for those reasons, I am just like you, your husband or wife, or a friend who likes to hunt, fish, and have adventures in the outdoors. Both out of curiosity and interest, and in some cases, a little bit of necessity, I decided that I wanted to learn how to cook what I brought home—from the outdoors or from the market—and have enjoyed every aspect of it. Now I want to share my experiences, hopefully in ways that will be fun and inspiring, and will help you and those you love get even more out of your lives outdoors.

As the idea for the content of this book began to come together, it became clear that "just another cookbook"—even one that focuses on wild fish and game rather than their domestic counterparts—would probably not generate much interest and that an approach that differed from other wild game cookbooks would be essential. Once you've experienced the seas, beaches, forests, and plains of North and Central America with me, I'm confident you'll agree that this book, in fact, takes quite a different approach!

First, you'll find a series of stories that relate actual outdoor adventures I've been fortunate enough to experience over the past forty-four years. From pursuing a wide spectrum of birds, fish, and small- and big-game quarry, to beachcombing with my wife and children, I've truly been blessed by being able to be in and enjoy firsthand the beauty and bounty of the natural world around us all.

Second, you'll note that each story features a complete meal menu and the associated recipes at its conclusion. The message, and intent, here is to relate adventures about one or more particular species, then help you with ideas as to how to prepare them for the table in ways that are both appetizing and visually appealing. I have never been a "trophy" hunter or fisherman. If I take off in pursuit of an animal or fish, it's more likely than not that my end objective is to put it on the table, and I hope that the stories and recipes shared in this book will encourage you to do the same.

Third, there are complete meal menus of complimentary dishes rather than single dishes that you have to decide how to combine with other items to make a complete meal. While there are a number of excellent wild fish and game recipe and/or cookbooks available today, very few "connect the dots" between the dishes made with the animal you harvested and other elements of a meal that complement each other. This approach allows me to help you, and your families and guests find the idea of eating wild game more appetizing. We've all heard about the nutritional benefits of eating wild game—low or no cholesterol, no chemicals or hormones, and little or no fat— but improper preparation and/or pairing of the game with other elements of a meal can take away from those benefits as well as from the overall experience.

Finally, the recipes and menus are, with only a few exceptions, fairly simple and straightforward. That is, you should be able to prepare meals that your friends and families will enjoy even if you aren't an expert in the kitchen, and your friends and family members aren't used to eating wild game. There are a couple of recipes that take extra time and care, and a couple that are a little more complex than others due to the subtlety of flavors or texture of the game, but I am confident that you can prepare every one of these recipes with some planning and care.

A parallel theme that also helped define the content of this book—from the stories themselves to the recipes that the stories introduce—is that of an enjoyment and appreciation of the outdoors and the bounty it has to offer. In some cases, sadly, the harvests I have described can no longer be experienced due to declining populations of the particular fish or game, or laws and regulations in force today that were not in effect at the time of the adventure that limit (or prohibit) the taking of the target species. Overall, though, those of you who are outdoor adventurists should be able to "relive" for yourselves the memories shared herein, and then be able to prepare and enjoy a meal of your harvest.

One thing you won't find in this book is the 'exception' or 'work-around' for the gamey or fishy taste some hunters or diners may have experienced. Call me lucky, perhaps, but I have never had a gamey- or fishy-tasting meal when the animal harvested was handled properly in the field and, subsequently, in the kitchen. Even traditionally wild-tasting meats—mountain goat, venison from an old buck mule deer, and Spanish mackerel, to name a few—are delicious if the proper care is taken with them in the field and, later, in the kitchen. That said, if you know or suspect that a particular animal won't be palatable, please think twice about killing it! In any event, most gamey or fishy flavors can be dealt with effectively through menu and ingredient selections. This book doesn't necessarily cover a wide gamut of recipes for each fish or game species, but you will find that the selections provided are based on experience that will help you make the most of whatever species you bring home.

Separately, you'll be glad to know that in many instances, the game, upon which featured recipes are based, can be replaced with "domestic" or commercially available equivalents without completely sacrificing the intended essence. For example, chicken (both meat and liver, as appropriate) can be used in place of rabbit (meat and liver) and pheasant (meat). Partridge (meat) and lean cuts of pork can be used in lieu of wild boar. Venison backstrap may be easier to work with than mountain goat, and it's perfectly okay to use store-bought fresh fish and shellfish when wild specimens aren't available. But this is a book about wild game, so I truly hope that you can experience the recipes as they were intended!

You will also find that there are some instances in which a particular recipe can be paired with more than one species of animal. That's intentional—done to provide you with several options for either your harvest or a recipe you like and want to use with another species. For example, the Slow Roasted Wild Boar is also great for sheep, mountain goat, and venison; and the Spanish Mackerel Ceviche can be made with brown jack (crevalle), amberjack, and even (farm-raised) Atlantic salmon and steelhead. Just be sure to carefully adjust cooking times based on the substituted game.

Likewise, the salads and sides can certainly be mixed and matched as you see fit. The menu selections I've suggested work well together but are certainly not the only way to go! The Fennel Slaw, for example, will go very nicely with Smoke-Roasted Wild Turkey as well as the wild boar. Mix and match. Find combinations that work for you. Enjoying every aspect of *your* outdoor experiences is what this book is all about!

In closing, I hope you enjoy the stories and photos—independently from the recipes. They are all true (or as close to true as my middle-aged memory will allow), and I did my absolute best to share each of them with you in as interesting a way as possible. Where I had photographs of the adventure, they are included; where I didn't, I've located photos on various state Fish & Game and Parks Department websites to help complete the overall experience or foregone pictures altogether. I hope that—whether or not I was able to include pictures—as you read each story, you'll feel as though you were there with me and able to imagine the sights, sounds, feelings, and tastes that made each experience special.

Field and Kitchen Basics and Essentials

Every hunter or fisherman knows that proper handling and storage of wild game is essential to the taste and texture of the meat that eventually hits the plate. Sometimes time, weather, or other circumstances prevent us from doing everything exactly "by the book" at the time of the harvest. Often, not being able to do everything that needs to be done immediately won't diminish the quality of your harvest, but certain basic steps should always be observed.

The Essentials

Before we get into a discussion regarding the proper handling and storage of your harvests, it's important to address the importance of using the proper processing equipment, both in the field and at home. Based on my personal experience, there are five "must haves" to ensure efficient handling and quality results:

1. high quality and properly maintained knives and saws;
2. a clean, flat work surface in a clean environment;
3. storage materials that fit the job and the game being processed;
4. high quality and properly maintained processing and cooking equipment; and
5. fresh, high quality herbs, spices, and produce.

Can you get by without one, some, or all of these items? Of course. After all, most of us have, at some point in our lives, not had the means to purchase high quality equipment or the knowledge of how much better and easier the handling and cooking of our game would be with the right gear. But, hopefully, one of the reasons you are reading this book is to learn something you didn't know that will help you do things better. And if I do my job, you'll come away with new information and compelling reasons to use it! In that spirit, let's address these five "must haves" in more depth.

Equipment

High quality and properly maintained knives and saws are critical because they will enable you to field dress, skin, quarter, or debone your game quickly and efficiently either in the field or at home. If you don't keep your knife (or knives) sharp, the job will be slower and harder than it needs to be. Quartering a 250-pound mule deer with the 4-inch sheath knife that you just used to field dress it, for example, is way too hard—and none too sanitary! Or splitting the backbone of an antelope with your camp hatchet instead of a sharp, fine-toothed bone saw is both a pain in the rear end and will likely result in damaged or wasted meat. And as a last example, trying to fillet a trout with your not-very-sharp pocketknife can be done, but it probably won't be pretty!

For all of these reasons, and after years of trial and error—some of which resulted in lost meat—I now use a matched set of knives and saws, and I keep them razor sharp and clean at all times. The manufacturer has worked hard to design and produce equipment of high quality with which an outdoorsman can handle even the most difficult field dressing, skinning or filleting, and processing your harvest efficiently. Of course, there are several equipment manufacturers whose products are of high quality and are well designed for the tasks at hand. For example, when I am hunting big game, I also carry (because my wife bought them for me as birthday and Christmas presents thirty-plus years ago, and because they're excellent knives) a folding knife with a straight 4-inch blade, and exchangeable gutting and serrated blades, as well as a fixed-blade skinning knife if I intend to keep the hide. Regardless of the brand, having tools designed for the job at hand will help you bring your harvest to the table with little or no wastage!

I also recommend—unless, of course, you are very experienced in processing your own game—that you obtain books and videos that explain proper field dressing and quartering, and final processing of the game you intend to harvest. For example, after thirty-plus years thinking that I was a pretty capable "butcher" of the big game I harvested, I purchased and watched a couple of game processing videos and learned that some of the techniques I had been using weren't quite right, and that there were some new things I could do to dramatically increase my processing efficiency. Even old dogs like me are willing to learn new tricks when it makes our lives easier!

Processing Environment

It should go without saying that a clean, well-lit work area with a large, flat surface is essential for processing your harvests—be they crustaceans, mollusks, fish, fowl, or large or small game—but many people (including myself for many years) make do with card tables or a hastily cleared-off garage work bench! Either will work, but the amount of extra time and effort that results from having to make accommodations for inadequate size and/or stability (not to mention cleanliness) makes purchasing or constructing a right-sized worktable worth whatever expense and/or time and effort required!

So what should you purchase or construct? I have found that a three-foot by six-foot hard-plastic table with folding legs and a flat work surface positioned under a three-foot fluorescent light provides ample workspace, light, and an overall environment that makes processing virtually anything I bring home easy. This assumes, of course, that a large animal, such as a mule deer, elk, or other similar-sized critter will have been quartered before being brought to the processing bench! The table can also be easily moved, if necessary, for outdoor washing, storage, etc.

Separately, if the fish or game I'm processing takes up a majority of the table's surface, I'll have a card table on which I put my wrapping and storage materials—butcher paper, aluminum foil, freezer bags, and the like—along with vinyl gloves, a bowl of warm water, and a clean towel.

A large cutting board is another key element of a well-equipped processing "station." However, it is extremely hard to find a cutting board that won't slip and slide on your hard plastic work surface, so I dampen towel that is larger than the cutting board and place the board on it before I begin. Another option is rubber matting—such as the material used to keep area rugs from sliding on hardwood or tile floors.

The cutting board itself should be "knife-friendly"—made of hardwood (oak, maple, hickory, etc.) or synthetic material that will not dull the blades of your knives. For that reason, I do not use bamboo or teak. They are excellent in the kitchen for both appearances and trimming vegetables, but they are very hard on your game processing equipment!

Finally, unless your processing table is close to the freezer in which you intend to store the processed game, you should have a clean cooler with plenty of ice close at hand. The problems that come with time and temperature can come into play while you're processing a large harvest, so be prepared to either keep the processed meat cool until you can get it into the freezer or take periodic breaks to put what you've processed into the freezer before continuing.

Storage Materials

Shellfish, fish, and meat will all last longer when they are properly processed and stored. One thing I learned—the hard way, through trial and lots of error, of course—is that having the right materials at hand before you begin processing your harvests is critical. High quality butcher or freezer paper and freezer-proof tape, along with a permanent-ink marking pen are must haves. Some butcher shops, grocery store delis, or meat counters will sell you a roll from their stock, but in any event, an Internet search will identify a number of online sources from which you can buy these supplies relatively cheaply, and each order should last you a season or more. Using freezer-proof paper will sever several purposes: first, it will prevent freezer burn, so storage life is extended and the quality of the meat will remain high. Second, it will allow you to wrap individual servings—one- or two-person portions or complete meals—and label them clearly so that it's easier to retrieve what you're looking for rather than having to guess! After wrapping the portions, I then store several at a time in zip-lock freezer bags and can remove them as needed, resealing the bag afterwards.

A good quality vacuum food sealer is another very useful tool that will pay for itself over time. Especially if you process several harvests (of any kind) per year, you'll be glad that you are able to protect them from freezer burn. Further, odd-sized and odd-shaped shellfish, fish, and game harvests that are clumsy to wrap in butcher paper are a breeze with a vacuum sealer.

I also use sealable plastic containers and half-gallon milk cartons filled with fresh, cold water when processing shellfish and fish. By freezing your catch in water, freezer burn is never an issue, and you can stack several containers neatly in your freezer.

Finally, I always make sure that I have an ample supply of heavy-duty plastic ziplock freezer bags and heavy-duty aluminum foil before I begin a large processing job. As mentioned earlier, several portions individually wrapped in butcher or freezer paper can be labeled and stored in a single one- or two-gallon freezer bag. Separately, I find that wrapping portions of smoked or cooked game in heavy-duty foil, then storing them in ziplock freezer bags is a convenient and effective way to go.

Processing Equipment

For the purpose of this section, "processing equipment" encompasses food processors, meat grinders, sausage stuffers, mixing bowls, and cookware. Your food preparation and cooking results just aren't going to be as good as they should be if you don't have and maintain clean, high-quality processing equipment. Obviously, if you know that you have no interest in making sausages, you may not need to invest in a sausage stuffer. That said, a meat grinder could also be used to process other kinds of food: potatoes for gnocchi, squash for risotto, etc.; and a sausage stuffer can, in fact, be used to make manicotti and other stuffed pasta dishes. My wife and I were fortunate enough to have a friend find a twenty-five-year-old Kitchen Aide mixer with meat grinder and sausage stuffer attachments, and we use it quite often to grind both wild and store-bought meats for pates, sausages, burgers and to stuff pasta shells.

It is also critical that the grinder and stuffer—including each of the components that are exposed to food materials—be thoroughly cleaned with strong soap and hot water, then dried, wrapped and stored in as sterile a condition as possible. Further, they should be washed and dried again before each use.

As for mixing bowls, I recommend (i) a set of sturdy, nonreactive (i.e., microwave-proof plastic or glass) bowls of 1, 2, 4 and 6 quarts each; plus (ii) a plastic, flat-bottomed 3- to 4-gallon tub (into which ground meats can be seasoned and mixed prior to making sausage). "Nonreactive" means that the material with which the bowls are made will not interact with salts, acids, enzymes, or other chemicals that frequently come into play when soaking or marinating meats, or when mixing various ingredients during cooking.

Selecting cookware tends to be a matter of personal preference: weight, balance, exterior color (to match the kitchen and other appliances), and other factors often come into play. To consistently put high quality food on the table for you, your family, and your guests to enjoy, however, you will be very happy if you purchase a few basic pieces:

- a 9-inch diameter, heavy-bottomed anodized sauté pan;
- a 12-inch diameter, heavy-bottomed, oven-proof anodized sauté pan;
- a 1-quart sauce pan;
- a 4-quart soup pot;
- a 6-quart or larger stock pot;
- a 9-inch by 12-inch (oven-proof) glass or aluminum casserole dish; and
- a 4- to 6-quart steel (lidded) roasting pan.
- Likewise, kitchen knives are tools that each chef must choose for themselves. Before you do so, however, consider the following basic ground rules when selecting your knives:
- First, each should be of high quality steel so you can sharpen it quickly and easily and so that it will hold the edge.
- Second, I use and recommend four basic styles that will help you handle most meals:
  - a) a slicing and scoring knife with a 5-inch blade;
  - b) at least one Santuko knife with a 5- or 6-inch blade (I have three Santukos with 3-inch, 4-inch, and 7-inch blades; and I use them constantly— particularly to slice, chop, and mince vegetables);
  - c) a chef 's knife with at least a 6-inch blade (I prefer an 8-inch blade to accommodate large roasts and the like);
  - d) a cleaver with a 6-inch blade; and
  - e) a high-quality sharpener.
- Third, hold and get the feel of each knife to the extent possible before buying it. While most stores will allow you to return or exchange a knife that hasn't been used, once you've used it, it's yours. Trying to use a knife that is clumsy, too light, or too heavy, or doesn't meet your expectations can result in handling errors and accidents.

Because you will want to protect your investment in these high-quality tools, and because you need to make sure that they are not used by anyone else who snuck into your kitchen and doesn't know how seriously they can cut the user, I recommend that you hang a 12- to 15-inch magnetic bar on the wall in a recessed area of your kitchen and store these knives separately from your other "everyday" kitchen knives and tools. They are expensive to replace if damaged through misuse, and they can be very dangerous if used by someone who is not used to handling very sharp instruments, so treat them accordingly. As a quick emphasis of this point, my wife and I have agreed that she will not use my good knives. She has a tendency to not pay close attention to what she's doing and has cut herself several times with my razor-sharp instruments; and she has misused them on occasion, requiring extra time and effort to return them to the proper condition.

Alternatively, you can store your knives in a wood knife block— with the sharp edge of the blade turned upward (i.e., so that they are not resting on the sharp edge). This will help avoid blunting of the blade, but also presents the opportunity for an accident if you forget or someone else is unaware that the blade is facing upward! In any event, I recommend that the block be kept separate from any other knife blocks for both protection and safety reasons.

Fresh, high-quality herbs and spices are essential. Generally speaking, a decent selection of herbs and spices can be bought in a well-stocked grocery store, but ordering online may yield a better result for those of you in the country or without access to a good selection. My wife and I currently have over sixty herbs and spices in our kitchen, and we'll use most of them at least once every month or two, but you can prepare all of the meals in this book with the following basics:

- *salts:* kosher and grey sea salt
- *peppers:* tellicherry (black) and white—medium ground
- *garlics:* fresh, granulated, and garlic salt
- *basil:* fresh, and dried and ground*
- *rosemary:* fresh, and dried and ground
- *thyme:* fresh, and dried and ground

- *ginger:* fresh, and dried and ground
- *chilies:* mild and medium heat, dried and ground
- *juniper berries:* whole, and dried and ground
- *cinnamon:* sticks and ground
- *lemon zest:* dried and ground
- *cloves:* whole, and dried and ground
- *allspice:* ground
- *Italian seasoning:* dried and ground
- *curries:* mild and medium heat
- *paprika:* Spanish and smoked

You should also keep these basic ingredients stocked:

- *oils:* extra virgin olive, canola, and sunflower
- *canned tomatoes:* diced, stewed, sauce, and paste
- *anchovies:* paste and tinned
- *rice:* wild, brown, and medium-grained white
- *flour:* all-purpose white and whole wheat
- *pasta:* whole grain spaghetti, linguini, and spiral
- *asiago or parmesan cheese:* fresh
- *soup base or stock:* chicken, beef, and veal

* Rebecca Gray makes an excellent suggestion that an easy way to have fresh herbs on hand is to buy potted plants available in many grocery stores and keep them on your counter or windowsill, plucking a leaf or two as needed, then replacing them when all of the leaves have been plucked.

Regarding measuring cups/spoons, all I'll suggest is that the tools you select are easy to read, easy to use (i.e., *not* hanging from a ring or loop), and that you have at least two full sets. I can't tell you how many times a menu has required measures of the same quantities of dry ingredients (flour, spices, etc.) and liquids (oil, water, cream, etc.), thus requiring me to pause to wash and dry the measuring tool before moving on! For a very nominal cost, you'll be very glad to have at least two sets at your fingertips!

Finally, I'll likewise leave the selection of cooking spoons, scrapers and the like to you with one simple comment: make sure that the spoons, etc., you use are heatproof. Many soft-plastic spoons and scrapers, for example, will melt if they are left in the pan—even when they're sitting in a sauce or other liquid base. A set of wood tools— especially bamboo—is versatile and heatproof (unless, of course, you leave them on a hot burner or in the oven), and several makes of silicon-based tools are available. Separately, because bacteria can live in furrows of wooden tools, be sure to clean them thoroughly with soap, hot water, and, occasionally, bleach after using them.

Handling Your Harvest

Crustaceans and mollusks

Time and temperature are the most critical considerations when bringing crustaceans (including lobster, shrimp, and crab) and mollusks (clams, geoducks, and mussels) from the beach or ocean to the table. If you plan an outing with the intention of harvesting any of these delicate-fleshed creatures, prepare properly by bringing a bucket or cooler of cool, even ice-cold, water. Of course, the water and the ice can be kept separate, allowing you to add a few cubes of ice from time to time to help stretch your supply, but the sooner you get your catch rinsed and into cool water, the less likely it will be to experience spoilage. A lid or cover for the cooler or bucket is also a good idea so as to slow the time it takes for the water temperature to increase. If your plans are to be in the "wild" for a long period of time, you should take occasional breaks to run your catch back to a large holding vessel once in a while.

Once your harvest is complete, it's just as important to get your harvest from its natural environment to where you can transition it from the cool water to the table, refrigerator, or freezer in a timely manner. As soon as practicable, on a clean kitchen counter or sink, or at your clean worktable, re-rinse your catch in cold, fresh water, then process them for eating or storage.

My experience with clams is that they should only be frozen if vacuum-sealed, and that they should not be refrigerated for more than twenty-four to thirty-six hours. Most clams are served immediately after being steamed until their shells open (and if their shells don't open after two or three minutes of steaming, they should not be eaten). But the "body" can also be removed from the shell, plunged into an ice-water bath, and stored in clean, fresh or lightly salted water in a tightly sealed container for up to three days.

Fish

As with crustaceans and mollusks, time and temperature are critical to maintaining the freshness and quality of fish. Fish should be "gilled" (by cutting out the gills) or "tailed" (by cutting off the tail) but not cleaned—and thus have their flesh exposed to airborne bacteria and heat—until or unless they can be stored in ice or ice-water, or wrapped and refrigerated immediately. Whenever I go out with a guide or on a charter boat, I ask how the catch will be stored until we return to port. On the outing described in "Cruisin' in Costa Rica," for example, I was pleasantly surprised to have our deckhand tell us that he always "gills" and bleeds, then cleans and fillets the catch within a few minutes of bringing it on board. He said that he always had a reservoir of cold, fresh water on board with which to wash his hands, the fillets, and the surfaces on which he fillets the fish, and always had a large cooler of fresh, clean ice and clean plastic ziplock bags so that he could store the fillets immediately after he cleaned them. This kind of care ensured that our catch was going to be of the highest quality when we returned to the resort.

Sometimes, space and other factors prevent that degree of planning and care, and, your fish probably won't suffer as a result. In such instances, my strong recommendation is to leave the fish whole and un-gutted (to avoid exposing the flesh to the air), and store it in as cool a container or spot as possible. That is, if you have room for a cooler of ice, use it. If you don't have room for a cooler, store the fish in a shady spot and rinse it with cool water as often as possible.

Birds

You've probably seen or read about our forefathers' method of handling game birds after the hunt—they hung the birds, usually by the neck, for several days. Modern science has taught us that you shouldn't do that! A host of bacteria, including E. coli from a bird's intestinal tract, as well as mites from the bird's feathers, will have a chance to taint the meat while it is aging.

In fact, leaving a bird uncleaned for more than twenty-four hours in temperatures of fifty degrees or more risks spoilage. At the end of a day's hunt, you should dress, skin, rinse, and put your birds on ice. Then, if you believe that aging your birds improves their flavor, clean and rinse them thoroughly, then hang them in a cool, dry, and clean place as you would a larger animal.

Personally, though, I am of the opinion that aging bird meat doesn't improve its texture or flavor. In fact, I much prefer making sure that the birds I harvest aren't allowed to dry out after cleaning. Marinating and/or seasoning them as needed to offset any toughness or gaminess will yield good, consistent results at the dinner table.

Many people discard the wings, thighs, and legs of wild birds, but (unless they've been badly damaged by shot pellets) the thighs, at the very least, can provide an extra dimension in texture and flavor to many dishes. Alternatively, you can save them to use in soup, sausage, and pates; so don't waste this excellent part of your birds!

Small game

Small game should be handled essentially the same as birds. They should be cooled—and kept cool—as soon as possible after being killed, and they should be cleaned and rinsed thoroughly within twenty-four hours (or less if the temperature exceeds fifty degrees). Once cleaned and rinsed, the animals can be stored on ice or in the refrigerator or freezer whole or quartered, at your discretion. Also, if you like chicken livers—sautéed, deep-fried, or in a pate—rabbit liver is an excellent alternative. Properly cleaned and preserved, rabbit liver is mild and full of both Vitamin D and "good" cholesterol, so don't forget to save it when you process your rabbit harvest!

Large Game

Fortunately for hunters in most states, big-game hunting seasons occur in the fall and early, when temperatures are generally lower than the rest of the year. This is, of course, to reduce hunting pressure during the animals' most stressful times of the year: winter—when forage is less nutritious and harder to find, spring—when animals give birth to their young, and summer—when the young grow and the older members of the herd eat plentifully in preparation for the coming breeding season and the hardships of winter.

One of the coincidental benefits of fall and early winter hunting seasons is that proper treatment and handling of harvested animals is easier, with less meat spoilage or loss to heat far less likely. The most southern states—Florida, Georgia, South Carolina, Alabama, Mississippi, Louisiana, Texas, New Mexico, Arizona, and southern California—are typically exceptions, with fall and early winter temperatures often remaining at fifty degrees and higher. Even in these states, however, proper planning and attention to the basics of field dressing and prompt processing will help keep your game from spoilage.

While an entire book could be written about proper handling and processing of your big-game harvest from the field to the locker to the freezer, I would rather hit on a few basics and refer you to some excellent material already available—starting with *The Art of Wild Game Cooking* by Eileen Clarke and Sil Strung. In their book, Ms. Clarke and Ms. Strung provide an extremely detailed and thorough discussion covering the nuts and bolts of handling and processing big-game animals. Separately, Outdoor Edge Corporation has produced the *Advanced Wild Game Processing* series of DVDs that take you from quartering and boning your animal to sausage making and beyond.

As for the basics—many of which are also addressed in *The Art of Wild Game Cooking* and *Advanced Wild Game Processing*—we'll focus here on the do's and don'ts of skinning, proper cooling of the carcass and meat, aging, and processing. Having a good grasp on these elements of big-game processing and handling will assure you of excellent results in the kitchen.

Skinning. In *The Art of Wild Game Cooking*, the authors make the observation that by skinning an animal in the field, the hunter has "removed the animal's own sterile game bag and replaced it with a manmade one, one that is not nearly as sturdy and will not keep the carcass from drying out." Further, anything other than a good muslin game bag will not keep bugs out, so what does skinning in the field accomplish? (Speaking from personal experience, one important benefit is that you won't expose young children to the "horror" of having to watch the process—even by accident.)

So unless you can butcher (process) the animal immediately or get the carcass to a cool storage locker to hang for aging, my advice is to field dress the animal and rinse the cavity as thoroughly as possible with clean water, but leave the animal in its skin. Once you are in a position to hang or butcher your harvest, you can then skin it and remove any remaining debris, cut out any bloodshot or tainted meat, and move to the next step.

Proper cooling. Moving to Georgia in 1999, I had to make several adjustments to my planning and approach to handling big game once I had it on the ground. When hunting feral pigs and deer in temperatures frequently in excess of seventy degrees, several accommodations helped make sure that the meat didn't suffer from spoilage due to heat:

- As soon after the kill as you can, field dress the animal and spread the chest cavity as wide as possible, then rinse it thoroughly to remove blood and any dirt or debris that may have made its way into the cavity during field dressing. Doing so will remove any undesirable body fluids—bile, intestinal material, etc.—and will start the cooling process;
- Have a source of fresh water reasonably close at hand. For example, when harvesting A Mixed Bag, my hunting buddy and I were able to take our deer to the shores of Banks Lake within a couple of hours of field dressing to wash out the animals' body cavities. Later, when hunting the Savannah National Wildlife Refuge in "Three Little Piggies," we were always near fresh water creeks or the Savannah River in which we would be able to rinse out the body cavities of our game as soon as possible after the kill. When hunting far inland, in areas where no water is readily available, I carry several one-gallon plastic milk jugs full of fresh water in the back of the car or truck and rinse out the body cavity as soon as possible. As mentioned earlier, a fresh water rinse will clean out dirt and body fluids that can increase the likelihood of spoilage and help cool the carcass; and
- Skin the animal as soon as possible, but not before you are ready and able to move to the next step—hanging or butchering. Especially if the temperature is below fifty degrees, you are not likely to suffer meat spoilage for twenty-four to thirty-six hours.

Aging. Aging meat has been a done for hundreds of years, even though the science behind it is not that old. Aging is, at its basest level, the process by which the collagen in meat is broken down by the enzymes that are also present in the meat, thus tenderizing it. If the animal you've harvested has little or no collagen, all the aging in the world will not make it more tender! Know, also, that the higher the average temperature during the aging process, the quicker the process will occur, so more attention—starting with regular inspection of the carcass to identify mold or odors—is essential. Butchering should be done immediately if any mold or even the faintest unpleasant odors are noted.

Generally, at average temperatures of forty-five to fifty degrees, a deer will have aged sufficiently in four to five days. Colder temperatures allow and require a little more time, and warmer temperatures will speed up the process. Finally, if the air temperature is going to average below freezing, you will need to heat the area in which the carcass is hanging to keep it warmer—at least thirty-five to forty degrees is a good rule of thumb—or the aging process may stop completely.

I have never intentionally aged the big game I've harvested, and the meat has always been flavorful and tender. What I didn't realize until reading *The Art of Wild Game Cooking* was that, in fact, the animal was aging without me realizing it or thinking of it as aging between the time rigor mortis left the body and when it was processed. In almost all cases, excluding the very young and tender feral hogs we butchered the afternoon of the hunt, my animals have been aged—prior to skinning—anywhere from ten to twelve hours to two days until I could process them.

Processing

As suggested earlier, I strongly recommend that anyone who processes their own big game obtain books or videos on the subject. Videos, in particular, give you the opportunity to watch the process being performed by an expert, and will, I assure you, either teach you things you didn't know or correct things you may have been doing wrong—or both! From quartering and deboning to the actual butchering process, using the proper techniques will ensure that you are able to save more meat and do more with that meat. As one quick example, *Advanced Game Processing* shows how to section out a hind leg differently than I had ever done it, yielding a couple of excellent roasts that I had never known how to "extract." The amount of meat was the same, but I was able to do more with what I had.

Once at the processing table with your game and your equipment in place, you're the boss. That is, you can butcher and package your fish, bird, or animal any way you want, based on what you intend to do with the meat. Here are a few suggestions as to what you can do for different needs:

Fish

- *Panfish.* In the South, panfish such as crappie, bream, perch, and the like are generally cooked whole; so processing them is easy. Gut, behead, and rinse the fish thoroughly in fresh water, then freeze them in milk cartons filled with fresh water. Plastic bags and foil are not recommended because the fish's sharp fins will puncture them, exposing the fish to freezer burn.
- *Medium to large fish.* Most medium to large freshwater fish: walleye, catfish, bass, pike, and trout (to name a few); and many saltwater fish: rockfish, ling cod, Cabezon, greenling, sea bass, crevalle, and the smaller species of tuna (again, to name a few) lend themselves to being filleted: gutted, then cut along each side of the backbone down to the rib bones, then along the rib bones to the bottom of the body cavity. There is a row of bones that protrudes up from the backbone at about a 45-degree angle into the fillet, leaving you the option of removing those bones with a pair of pliers or leaving them in place. If you leave them, be sure to warn your guests! Note: the only bones present from the tail end of the body cavity to the tail are the vertical bones of the backbone, so a tail section fillet is always boneless.

- *Large fish.* There are additional options available when processing large freshwater and saltwater fish depending on how you intend to prepare them.

    For example, virtually any large fish, from lake trout, musky, salmon, medium-to-large tuna, swordfish, amberjack, etc., can be portioned into steaks by cutting at a 90-degree angle to the fish. If you plan to cut your lake trout, salmon, or tuna into steaks, my recommendation is that you fillet the tail section (i.e., from the tail end of the body cavity down to the tail), then cut the rest of the fish into steaks of no more than one inch in thickness.

    If you plan to smoke your trout, salmon, Spanish or king mackerel, etc., you'll get the best results from filleting them, then cutting the fillets into manageable pieces before brining or marinating them. Here again, you can either remove the bones that remain in fillets before smoking or leave them to deal with at the table.

Birds

    With very few exceptions, I am of the opinion that game birds can be best handled and processed by field dressing and skinning, then removing the head and neck, the wings above the "elbow" (i.e., the first joint), and the legs at the hip joint. Then the legs should be cut at the "knee" to make two pieces, and the remaining wing section should be severed from the body at the "shoulder." These pieces can then be stored separately for use in soups, sausages, *coq au vin*, and other dishes in which they will be cooked to the point of falling off the bone.

    That said, if you know in advance that you want to roast a whole bird, remove the feet by cutting them off at the joint below the drumstick, and remove the wings by cutting them off at the elbow joint. You should then pluck all of the feathers, taking care to avoid allowing feathers into the body cavity. Unless you have (or have access to) a plucking machine as we did in "Mostly Mallards," plucking can be tedious and time-consuming. As one approach, some people pluck the large outer feathers, then finish off the remaining under feathers or down with a propane or butane torch by flash searing them, then wiping against the grain with a towel to remove the residual ash and stubs. Chances are that you will not eat the skin after cooking, so this method works well and saves a lot of time. Either way, once you've finished plucking the bird, remove the head and neck before wrapping or packaging.

If you skin the bird and remove the wings and legs, you then need to deal with the breast by either removing each side carefully from the breastbone and ribs with a sharp fillet knife, or cutting laterally through the ribs to remove the backbone. In the latter case, the breast can either be cooked whole or boned out (filleted) prior to cooking.

Small Game

The simplest and, generally, most effective way to process small game such as rabbits, squirrels, and other similarly-sized animals is as follows:

- field dress and rinse before bringing them to your processing table;
- skin;
- remove the head just below the skull and the feet at the elbows and knees;
- quarter as you would a big-game animal, removing the front legs at the shoulders and the hind legs at the hips;
- remove the lower half of the rib cage by cutting laterally across the ribs just below the bottom of the backstraps; and
- cut the body in half just below the rib cage. Even if the amount of meat on the lower half is small, it will provide plenty of flavor to the sauce, or can be used to make stock.

Large Game

As we've discussed previously, I heartily recommend that you obtain a book or DVD that walks you through the processing of large game, but I can recommend a few basics in processing your animals:

- field dress and thoroughly rinse the body cavity with clean, fresh water;
- if circumstances are such that bringing the animal out in pieces is necessary, skin it—either after hanging it in as cool a place as possible or by skinning it on one side then rolling it over, still on the skin, and skinning the other side—then "quarter" the animal.

In true quartering, you'll need to: (i) split the chest open at the sternum, (ii) split the backbone down the center from the hips to the neck (or carefully cut the backstraps along the backbone and cut the ribs from the backbone using either a bone saw or a hatchet), and then (iii) cut the body in half by cutting through the backbone just below the rib cage. Voila—four quarters!

For a large mule deer, elk, moose, or caribou, however, quartering involves cutting the animal into more than four pieces due to size and weight considerations. When dealing with these larger species:

(i) remove the front legs at the shoulders, (ii) remove the back legs at the hips, (iii) remove the tenderloins, (iv) remove the neck by cutting crosswise just above the front of the rib cage, (v) split the chest open at the sternum, (vi) cut the body in half by cutting through the backbone just below the rib cage, and then (vii) split the backbone down the center from where you cut the body in half to the neck (or carefully cut the backstraps along the backbone and cut the ribs from the backbone using either a bone saw or a hatchet and discard the backbone.

- If you can transport the animal whole, cool the body cavity as much as possible by opening up the rib cage and using ice if the air temperature is above fifty-five degrees;
- Skin the animal once it is in a clean and moderately controllable environment—relative to bugs, rodents, and temperature;
- Age the skinned carcass by hanging it for a period of time consistent with the animal's age and body size, and with the air temperature between thirty-five to forty degrees and fifty degrees; and
- When the meat is sufficiently aged, proceed with butchering, removing, and processing section of the animal at a time.

I realize that this overview doesn't come close to covering everything that a person new to hunting and/or cooking wild game needs to know, and that a veteran hunter and/or wild game cook probably already has their own views and approaches to certain techniques used to process and cook their harvests. In either case, my intention is to offer some ideas that may be helpful to anyone who loves the outdoors and its bounties.

So with these thoughts and suggestions in mind, let's venture outdoors to harvest some critters and see what we can do with them!

Hare Triggers!

Only a few of the farmers my parents and I met when we asked for permission to hunt their property had kids (or at least, kids my age). Fortunately, we met and became friends with a farm family that owned a large farm south of Othello, Washington, in prime pheasant hunting country, so we hunted there frequently. Their younger son, Gary, was a precocious ten-year-old; and because I was also ten, we hit it off immediately!

Two years after we met Gary's family, our folks agreed to allow Gary and I to each spend a week with the other's family. I got to go first, in late June 1968. When I arrived, Gary's folks welcomed me warmly, then laid out a number of chores for Gary and I to do each day: feeding the chickens and collecting eggs, feeding the pigs, and tending to the vegetable garden. No big deal, but by the time we finished them each morning, we were raring to get on with our own adventures!

The temperatures in eastern Washington in late June usually reach the mid to high seventies, so by lunchtime, after hunting for pigeons in the barn rafters with our BB guns, it was hot. One evening after dinner, though, Gary proposed a new plan for the next day. "Let's go rabbit hunting!" he whispered.

I didn't think our BB guns had enough power to kill a rabbit, or that we could get close enough to the skittish critters for a killing shot; but we were ten, so we didn't sweat the small stuff!

The next morning, we did our chores quickly so that we could get our hunt underway. We fed the chickens and gathered eggs, fed the pigs, and finally made our way to the garden to pick some tomatoes. When we had finally finished, we grabbed our guns and headed for a brushy draw on the west end of the farm.

Although this rabbit hunt was a first for both of us, Gary was sure that we'd be able to find a few. Probably looking more like Elmer Fudds than real hunters, we crept, guns at the ready, along the edges of the draw in hopes of having a rabbit sprint out of the cover onto the dirt road paralleling the draw. We actually saw a couple of cottontails scurry from the road *into* the brush, but they were quick, and we weren't close enough for a shot.

At the bottom of the draw, we sat down on some aluminum irrigation pipes lying next to a barbed-wire fence to discuss our next move.

"Let's see if we can find some jack rabbits," Gary suggested, pointing to the open, sagebrush-covered hillside on the opposite side of the draw.

"Jackrabbits are *really* fast!" I responded, pretty sure by this time that the sun had cooked Gary's brain.

"Yeah, but if we crawl instead of walk, we might be able to sneak up on them," he countered, undaunted.

So off we went, crossing the shallow draw and making our way into the sagebrush. With about twenty yards between us, we started crawling across the hillside. My knees had started to ache when a large gray long-eared jackrabbit burst out from under a small tumbleweed.

"I almost had a shot at him!" Gary hissed just loud enough for me to hear him. "I'll get the next one, though!"

A few minutes later, I saw one of the large rabbits sitting motionless beside a sage bush, and I carefully raised my gun to my shoulder. Just as I began to squeeze the trigger, I heard Gary's gun pop, and the hare took off in a streak.

"I think I hit him!" Gary said from the cover to my left. "Nope. You hit a branch just in front of him," I responded. "Dang it!" he called back.

By the time we got to the fence line on the far side of the hill, we had seen seven jacks. We had each taken two shots from less than twenty yards, so getting close was proving to be easier than we had expected, but we still hadn't endangered the lives of any of the speedsters!

Once we had rested, we crept slowly down the fence line until we were nearly to the bottom of the hill. Gary stopped and whispered that he would start from that point and said that I should keep going to where the sagebrush gave way to the grass next to the road. By this time, the heat had peaked and we were sweating, but a gentle breeze helped a little.

We had crawled almost fifty yards when I saw a cottontail feeding at the edge of the thick grass. I could see Gary to my right and signaled him to freeze. Slowly, I brought my gun to my shoulder, took careful aim, and squeezed off the shot. Unfazed, the rabbit dove into the deep grass.

"What happened?" Gary asked as he raised his head above the brush.

"My gun doesn't have enough power!" I told him.

"Keep trying. Maybe you'll get lucky!" he replied, dropping back to his hands and knees.

A few minutes later, I heard Gary's gun pop, and he shouted jubilantly, "I got him! I got a jackrabbit!"

Racing to where it lay, Gary picked it up by the hind legs—its ears nearly touching the ground as he held it at shoulder level.

Jackrabbit – Photo courtesy of the Texas Dept. of Fish & Wildlife

A few minutes after we resumed our crawl, I saw another cottontail and, from a mere twelve feet, shot the unsuspecting rodent just behind its eye. It flopped, kicking, on the ground, then lay still. "I knew you could do it!" Gary said gleefully as I held the rabbit up for him to see.

"I believe you—now!" I grinned back.

Cottontail – Photo courtesy of the Kansas Dept. of Wildlife

When we finished our crawl, dragging our prizes as we went, we had seen two more jackrabbits, but neither of us was able to get close enough to take an ethical shot, however. Even so, we were very pleased with the results of our efforts and were eager to get back to the house to get a cold soda and clean our harvest.

Gary's mom was less than overjoyed (but very polite) when we showed her the rabbits, and the braised dish she made for us the following night put the perfect finishing touch on Gary and Stan's excellent adventures!

Shiitake Mushroom Raviolis in Chicken Broth

Ingredients:

- pasta dough (recipe below) or 40 wonton wrappers, 3 in. in diameter
- 8 oz. of shiitake mushrooms; stems removed and reserved, then minced
- 4 tbsp. butter
- 1 shallot, peeled and minced
- 3 tbsp. fresh chives, minced
- kosher salt and coarsely ground black pepper, to taste
- 6 cups chicken soup base or stock
- ½ oz. dried porcini mushrooms
- 1 tsp. fresh Italian parsley leaves, minced
- 1 tsp. fresh thyme leaves, minced, or ½ tsp. dried leaves, crushed
- 2 tsp. whole black peppercorns
- 2 qt. water
- ½ tbsp. kosher salt

Preparation:

1. Heat the butter until it foams in a medium sauté pan over medium-low heat. Add the shallot and sauté until tender—8 to 10 minutes. Reduce the heat to low and stir in the shiitake mushrooms, then cover and cook until tender—10 to 15 minutes more. Add 2 tablespoons of the chives, plus salt and pepper to taste, stirring to mix completely.

2. If using pasta dough, use a 3-inch cookie cutter to cut the pasta into 40 circles (or if using wonton wrappers, lay out 40 circles) on a flat cutting board.

3. One at a time, brush the circles with water using a pastry brush. Place ½ to ¾ teaspoon of the mushroom mixture on each circle, then fold over, lining up the edges of the circle, and pinch or press the edges together with a small fork. Let the circles dry at least 30 minutes before cooking.

4. For the broth, combine the chicken soup base or stock, reserved shiitake stems, dried porcini pieces, parsley, thyme, and peppercorns in a 5-quart soup pot over medium-high heat. Bring the mixture to a boil, then reduce the heat to low and simmer, covered, for 20 minutes.

5. Remove the stock from the heat and let it cool for at least 15 minutes, then strain the entire mixture into another pan or bowl. Discard the strained ingredients. Reheat the broth while cooking the raviolis.

6. In a 4-quart stockpot, bring the water and 1 tablespoon salt to a boil. Working in batches, add the raviolis to the boiling

7. water and cook until they float to the surface, then cook for 1 minute longer. Transfer the cooked raviolis gently with a slotted spoon to individual serving bowls, then ladle the broth into each bowl.

8. Sprinkle the remaining chives into each bowl and serve immediately.

Pasta Dough

Ingredients:

- 1¼ cup semolina flour
- 2/3 cup unbleached, all-purpose flour, plus more for dusting
- ¼ tsp. kosher salt
- 2 eggs (at room temperature)
- 1½ tbsp. water

Preparation:

1. On a flat, clean work surface, combine the flours and salt in a mound. Make a crater in the center of the mound and break in the eggs. Add the water. Using a fork, blend the ingredients by stirring gently in a circular motion from the well outward, slowly drawing in the flour until all of the ingredients make a dough.

2. Dust the work surface with flour. Using a scraper and the palm and heel of your hands, knead the dough, working it down and away from you, and turning it frequently until the dough feels smooth—about 8 to 10 minutes. Sprinkle more flour onto the dough if it becomes sticky or soft. Cut the finished dough into 4 even pieces.

3. Working with each piece individually, place the dough on a freshly floured work surface and flatten it into a rectangle with your hand. Using a floured rolling pin, roll the dough away from you with moderate pressure. Turn the dough over and around, then repeat, adding more flour if the dough becomes sticky or soft.

4. Continue until the dough reaches the desired thickness. Repeat this process for each piece.

5. Cover your worktable with waxed paper and sprinkle lightly with flour. Place each sheet of pasta side by side on the paper and let them rest until they are dry to the touch but still soft—about 10 minutes.

Yam, Asparagus, and Pecan Salad with Maple Syrup and Brandy Dressing

Ingredients:

- 2 medium yams, peeled and chopped into
- 1-inch square cubes
- 1 qt. water
- 5 fresh asparagus stalks, woody stems removed, then cut into 1-inch pieces
- ¼ cup shelled and coarsely chopped pecans
- ¼ cup maple syrup*
- 2 tsp. coarsely ground black pepper
- 2 tbsp. brandy**
- Imitation maple flavored syrup, including sugar free, works fine

** Optional

Preparation:

1. Boil the yam cubes in water until just soft, then rinse under very cold water. Place in a salad bowl to cool completely.
2. Steam the asparagus pieces until just soft, then rinse under very cold water. Add to the salad bowl to cool completely.
3. Add the chopped pecans to the salad bowl.
4. In a separate small bowl, combine the maple syrup, pepper, and brandy, and mix thoroughly.
5. Pour the dressing over the yams, asparagus, and pecans, tossing gently.
6. Cover and refrigerate at least 2 hours before serving.

Garlic Sesame Asparagus

Ingredients:

- 1 pound asparagus, with woody stems removed
- ¼ cup sesame oil
- 1 Tbsp granulated garlic
- 2 Tbsp butter

Preparation:

1. Preheat oven to 425°F.
2. Wash and peel the asparagus.
3. Place the asparagus on a 12 inch baking sheet, sprinkle the garlic evenly, then drizzle the sesame oil over the top.
4. Transfer the pan to the oven, and bake for 15-20 minutes until the asparagus stems are tender and lightly browned.

Braised Rabbit in a Madeira Reduction

Ingredients:

- one 2–3 lb. rabbit, cleaned, skinned, and washed in cold water, then cut into 6 pieces*
- ¼ cup stone-ground mustard
- coarsely ground black pepper, to taste
- 1 tbsp. olive oil
- 3 shallots, sliced and chopped
- 2 tbsp. minced garlic cloves
- 1 tbsp. butter
- ¼ cup dry white wine
- ½ tsp. dried ground tarragon
- 1 cup chicken soup base (or low-sodium stock)
- ¼ cup Madeira
- ½ lb. fresh shiitake mushrooms, sliced
- ½ cup fat-free sour cream
- 1 tbsp. chopped fresh Italian parsley or basil leaves

*Front and back legs, plus body cut crosswise behind the rib cage.

Preparation:

1. Brush the rabbit pieces with mustard, then sprinkle with pepper. Set aside.
2. In a 9-inch skillet, heat 1 tablespoon of the oil over medium heat. Add the shallots and garlic, and sauté until the shallots are tender.
3. Add the butter and stir until it is melted, then add the rabbit pieces. Sauté until well browned on both sides.
4. Remove the rabbit pieces and add the wine. Stir and scrape the bottom of the pan to deglaze it as it cooks.
5. Return the rabbit pieces to the pan and add the tarragon, soup base, and Madeira. Reduce the heat and simmer, covered, until the rabbit is loose on the bone—about 45 to 50 minutes.
6. Move the rabbit pieces from the pan to a plate and cover loosely with aluminum foil.
7. Add the mushrooms to the pan and sauté in the liquid until it is reduced by two thirds. Add the sour cream and reduce until the sauce thickens. Season to taste.
8. Return the rabbit pieces to the sauce to reheat, then transfer to a platter. Spoon the sauce over the meat and garnish with the chopped parsley or basil.

Suggested Accompaniment

- *Merlot:* Chateau St. Michelle Indian Wells— Columbia Valley, Washington, or Simi— Sonoma Valley, California

Braised Rabbit in a Madeira Reduction

You Caught a What?

Catching Pacific rockfish was always a fun by-product of my family's salmon fishing trips to Neah Bay, Washington. One day in August 1968 turned out to be most unusual.

Our primary target would be a large run of pink salmon (also called "humpies" because of the way the males' backs hump up just behind the head as spawning time approaches). The reports in the newspaper said that the run was unusually strong that year, and Dad wanted us to get in on it!

Arriving in late afternoon, we set up our Apache tent trailer and prepared our camp-stove dinner. Dad was a little disappointed that we had arrived too late to go fishing that day, but we all walked to the docks and saw *lots* of humpies being unloaded from the boats coming in. Our plan was to fish from sun up until about 9:00 a.m., then come in for breakfast and a nap before heading back out in the early afternoon, and I dreamt about those fish until Dad woke Mitch and I the next morning.

Fog hung in the air, and the water was like glass as we rounded Waddah Island and entered the Strait of Juan de Fuca. Once into the Strait, Dad cut the outboard motor to an idle and began rigging our hooks with plug-cut herring. Suddenly, a school of herring shattered the glassy surface of the water beside us. Dad quickly dropped our baits into the water and shifted the motor into gear, guessing that the panicked herring had a school of salmon chasing them.

He was right, and within minutes, we each had fish on our lines. We boated three fat little humpies, quickly rebaited, and lowered our lines back into the bait school. We ended up back at the dock with our three-person limit of nine fish well before nine o'clock!

Pink Salmon – Image Courtesy of Washington Department of Fish & Wildlife

After breakfast, Mom and Dad let Mitch, Michale, and I walk down to the general store to paw through its racks of dried starfish, shells, and toys made by the local Makah Indians. We each bought souvenirs with our allowance money and returned to the trailer happy.

When Dad awoke from his nap, he asked, "Who wants to go fishing?" Surprisingly, I was the only taker, so he and I were quickly on our way toward the rocky shoreline northwest of town. We had both caught our daily limit of salmon that morning, so rockfish would be our only prey.

The water was very deep where we would be fishing, so anchoring wasn't an option. Dad positioned us about forty yards from a rocky outcropping and cut the motor, knowing that we'd drift a little and have to reposition after a while. We soon had our baited lines in the water, "mooching" by bouncing our five-ounce lead weights off the bottom, quickly reeling up about twenty feet, dropping the lead back down, and so on.

As it happened, we had found a great spot, and Dad and I each hooked and landed nice yellow-eyed rockfish, followed quickly by a pair of black sea bass.

Rockfish – Photo Courtesy of Alaska Department of Fish & Game

The tide and waves soon moved us almost a hundred yards. Dad cranked up the motor to move us back to where we started, and I rebaited our hooks. Within minutes of dropping our baits again, I hooked another fish. A kelp bed lined the rocks in front of us, so I knew I had to keep the fish out of the long, strong fronds. Dad set his rod in the pole holder and began coaching me. "Point your rod tip to the right when the fish runs away from you, and tighten your drag a little. He's not big enough to break you off unless he gets into the kelp or rocks, and tightening the drag will help make sure that doesn't happen." I, at the ripe old age of almost thirteen, didn't want him to help me fight the fish but knew his advice was right on!

After a short battle, I brought the fish to the boat. "What is it?" I said, gawking at the unusual-looking fish in the net. "It's called a cabezon," he replied. "They usually live further offshore, but they're really good for eating!"

Cabezon – Photo courtesy of Washington Department of Fish & Wildlife

"Mom will sure be surprised!" I grinned, happy to have caught a fish no one else in the family had ever seen.

Dad soon hooked another fish, working to keep it away from the kelp. As I netted the odd-looking fish, I asked, "What's this one?"

"It's a kelp greenling," he answered.

Kelp Greenling – Image Courtesy of Washington Dept of Fish & Game

"Have you ever caught one?" I asked.

"No, but Mr. Staples (one of our neighbors, who, with his family, had joined us on a few Neah Bay treks) caught one last year. He said it was really tasty."

"Mom will *really* be surprised to see *two* new kinds of fish!" I said.

He agreed, saying, "She'll be sorry she didn't come with us!"

An hour later, we had a dozen nice fish in the box and decided to head in. It was a beautiful afternoon, so we decided to take our time heading back to town. We saw other boats scattered along the way fishing for humpies, and occasionally saw a net hoisted into the air signaling that a fish had been hooked.

Approaching Waddah Island, we saw a boat with two fishermen playing a fish. "Let's see what they've got," Dad said as we got close enough to watch. It quickly became clear that they had hooked a large king salmon. As we watched, the fish made several runs, then rolled on the surface near our boat as it began to tire. "That fish is probably at least thirty pounds!" Dad exclaimed.

Almost as he spoke, a charter boat off to our right began to motor slowly on a course between us and the other fishermen. Realizing that the boat's prop would probably cut the line, we all began shouting and waving our arms.

"Grab the net," Dad said as he shifted our outboard into gear. He maneuvered us toward the tired fish and shifting into neutral, said, "Slide the net under it as soon as you can reach it." A moment later, the huge fish was in the net; and as we hoisted the fish into the boat, we saw the other fishermen reeling in their severed line.

Dad shifted our boat into gear again and headed for their boat.

"Did you see that jerk?" one of the men said as we came close enough to hear. "He ran over our line and we lost a great fish!"

Maybe not, Dad responded.

"What do you mean?" the man asked.

"We were able to net it!" I said, lifting enough of the net for them to see their fish.

"Holy cow!" the other fellow replied. "Thanks a lot, guys! You caught our fish!" he said.

"As a matter of fact," Dad said, smiling as we transferred the big salmon to their boat, "we caught a little of everything today."

Oriental Salad with Sesame Dressing

Ingredients:

- ¼ cup rice vinegar
- ¼ cup vegetable oil
- 1 tsp. sesame oil
- 2 tbsp. sugar
- ¼ tsp. kosher salt
- ¼ tsp. medium ground white pepper
- 3 cups bok choy, rinsed and torn or chopped coarsely
- 1 cup bean sprouts, rinsed
- ½ cup toasted cashews, coarsely chopped
- 1 ripe avocado, peeled, pitted, and cut into ½-inch cubes

Preparation:

1. Mix the vinegar, oils, sugar, salt, and pepper thoroughly in a nonreactive container
2. Place the bok choy, bean sprouts, cashews, and avocado in a serving bowl, pour half of the dressing over the top, toss gently. Repeat with the rest of the dressing, then serve.

Butternut Squash

Ingredients:

- 2 tbsp. butter
- 1 medium to large butternut squash, peeled, seeded, and cut into ¾-inch cubes
- ½ cup chicken soup base or stock
- ¼ cup water
- 1 tbsp. dark-brown sugar

Preparation:

1. Heat butter in a large skillet over medium-high heat until golden brown.
2. Add the squash and sauté, stirring occasionally, until golden brown and tender when pierced with a fork—about 18 to 20 minutes.
3. Add chicken broth, the water, and brown sugar; and cook until the liquid has evaporated and the squash caramelizes—about 5 to 7 minutes.
4. Remove from heat, season to taste with salt and pepper, transfer to a serving bowl, and serve with the steamed cabezon.

Steamed Pacific Cabezon with CranberryGinger Sauce

Ingredients:

- ½ cup warm water
- ¼ cup dried cranberries
- 1½ cups cold water
- 3 tbsp. orange juice
- 2 tbsp. dry sherry
- 1 tbsp. brown sugar
- 1 tsp. chopped or grated fresh ginger root
- four 6-oz. cabezon fillets

Preparation:

1. In a small bowl, cover the cranberries with ½ cup warm water and soak for at least 1 hour.
2. Transfer the cranberries to a small pan and add 1 cup of the cold water to cover and cook at medium-high heat until the cranberries are soft to the touch and the water has all but evaporated. Add the remaining ½ cup as needed to complete the cooking process. Reduce the heat to a simmer.
3. Add the orange juice, sherry, brown sugar, and ginger.
4. Cook until the mixture thickens to a syrupy texture, then remove from the burner and set aside.
5. Fill a stockpot large enough to accommodate a vegetable steamer basket with enough water to almost reach the bottom of the steamer basket.
6. Heat the water to simmering (but do not let it reach a full boil).
7. Place a piece of aluminum foil on the bottom of the steamer basket, then place four 6-oz. cabezon fillets side-by-side on the foil. Pour the lentil sauce over the fillets, then cover the pot.
8. Cook until the fillets are slightly firm to the touch but flake easily—about 20 minutes.
9. Remove the steamer basket from the pot, transfer the fillets to a plate, and serve immediately.

* Also excellent with Chilean seabass, ling cod, halibut, and other white-fleshed ocean fish.

Broccoli Florets with Garlic and Pimentos

Ingredients:

- 1 cup water
- 3 cups rinsed broccoli florets
- 3 garlic cloves, peeled and minced
- ¼ cup pimento slices
- 2 tbsp. butter
- kosher salt and coarsely ground black pepper, to taste

Preparation:

1. Bring the water to a boil in a medium saucepan with a steamer insert or basket.
2. Place the broccoli, garlic, and pimento slices in the steamer insert or basket, cover, and steam until the broccoli florets are tender—about 12 minutes.
3. Remove the pan from the burner and transfer the broccoli, garlic, and pimentos to a serving bowl. Add the butter and the salt and pepper, and serve with the steamed Cabezon.

Suggested Accompaniment

- *Pouilly Fuisse:* Lois Jadot—Burgundy, France
- *Sauvignon Blanc:* William Cole Columbine Reserve—Chile or Snoqualmie—Columbia Valley, Washington

Steamed Pacific Cabezon

Pheasants with a Phlair!

As most dedicated upland bird hunters will agree, a key ingredient to success is a trained pointing dog suited for the combination of thick cover and open terrain that bird hunters in Washington frequently encounter. Dad chose a white-and-liver German Shorthair we named Penny. She had both the gentle disposition of a family dog, and an innate nose and love of hunting that few dogs I've known since have matched.

Early in the 1967 hunting season, Dad asked me if I wanted to hitch up our Apache tent trailer and head southeast from Seattle over the Cascade mountains to the small farming communities of Royal City and Othello where we had struck up a relationship with a few families who let us camp and hunt on their farms. He didn't have to ask twice!

Because of their large leaves, sugar beets are a favorite daytime feeding and bedding area for pheasants, and we had always been able to find at least a few birds whenever we could get into a beet field. And because the beets were so thick, it was sometimes possible to hunt the same field for several hours, moving lengthwise up and back the first time, then cutting crosswise or even diagonally a couple more times before all of the birds were flushed out. In addition to being heavy and thick, the leaves of mature sugar beets stand two feet or more tall. But because the leaves stand fairly upright, the furrows in the ground between rows create tunnels in which the birds can hide and even run. As a fairly small dog, Penny had learned how to use the tunnels to follow a running bird, and had even caught several on past trips.

As we rolled slowly over the last rise on our way to a favorite field, we saw several rooster ringnecks dusting in the road ahead! Dad pulled to the side of the dirt road, and we quietly climbed out of the car, donned our gear, and got ready to enter the field.

Penny was full of energy and bounded into the beets as if she was a Springer spaniel—leaping nearly vertically with her ears flapping. Within moments—less than twenty yards into the field, she locked on point, her nose buried in the base of a beet plant. "Whoa!" Dad shouted, both to reassure Penny that we knew she had found a bird and to make certain that we were properly aware of each other as well as the dog.

Out from under the beet leaves, a bright rooster thundered, cackling. As it angled away to my left, I shouldered my side-by-side Fox-Savage 20-gauge shotgun, took aim down the barrels, and fired. The gun roared, but the bird kept flying! Recovering my balance from the first shot, I drew down on the bird again, this time leading it slightly. Bam! The second shot hit its mark, and the bird fell. Penny was off in a flash and quickly gathered the bird in her mouth.

No more than a minute later, and in spite of the ruckus caused by the first bird, Penny locked on point again. This time it was a hen, so we watched it flap and sail away from us. Penny found bird after bird, and by the time we reached the end of the field on our first pass, Dad had one bird, and I had two (because he usually tried to let me shoot first).

About midway up the field on our second pass, Penny again locked on point, and Dad again shouted, "Whoa," as we crept toward the hiding bird. This time, though, it had decided to run.

"Get it!" Dad told Penny, and off she went under the beet-leaf canopy. We couldn't see her, but we laughed as we watched the leaves shake and rustle as she tore after that bird. A few seconds later, we heard a tussle and saw dust rise from under the leaves; and Penny emerged with a majestic, crimson- and amber-breasted rooster locked firmly in her mouth. It kicked and scratched at her until Dad reached down and grabbed it from her. Just as he wrung its white collar, another rooster launched itself into the air directly behind us. Without saying a word, Dad handed me the first bird and rotated as he brought his 20-gauge Browning Lightning over-under shotgun to his shoulder. This bird was flying perpendicular to us almost thirty-five yards away, and Dad had a bead on it.

But before he could pull the trigger, another rooster took off almost directly behind me and headed the exact opposite direction. Bam! The first shot roared and the bird crumpled. "Mark it!" he shouted as it hit the ground. Then, in one continuous motion, he swung nearly 180 degrees to line up on the second bird. Bam! His gun roared and the second bird dropped like a rock. I was only twelve at the time, but I knew good shooting when I saw it, and that was great shooting! Making it look effortless, Dad had shot two birds, each at a fairly lengthy distance and flying in opposite directions. "That was amazing!" I managed to say. Being a modest guy, Dad didn't say anything, but his grin spoke volumes. Fortunately, Penny wasn't as easily impressed and took off after the first bird.

The beets didn't bother us as we walked back to the car with full vests and the memory of a fantastic hunt. Since that fall afternoon, I've hunted different kinds of birds many times and in many places, but Dad's "Pheasants with a Phlair" has always been one of my favorite memories.

Iceberg Lettuce Wedges with Creamy Gorgonzola Dressing

Ingredients:

- ¾ cup fat-free sour cream
- 1½ cups reduced-fat mayonnaise
- 4 oz. Gorgonzola cheese, crumbled
- 1 tsp. Worcestershire sauce
- 1 tsp. Dijon mustard
- ½ tsp. coarsely ground black pepper
- ¼ tsp. granulated garlic
- ¼ tsp. onion powder
- ¼ tsp. kosher salt
- 1 small- to medium-sized head of iceberg lettuce, cored and quartered vertically

Preparation:

1. Mix the sour cream, mayonnaise, cheese, Worcestershire sauce, mustard, pepper, garlic, onion, and salt thoroughly in a nonreactive mixing bowl. Refrigerate at least 1 hour before serving
2. Place each lettuce wedge on a salad plate and pour dressing over it. Serve immediately.

Aromatic Jasmine Rice

Ingredients:

- 2 tbsp. peanut oil
- 2 medium shallots, minced
- 2 cups jasmine rice
- 1 tsp. turmeric
- 1 tsp. ground coriander
- 1 whole cinnamon stick
- ½ tsp. kosher salt
- ½ tsp. cumin
- 3½ cups chicken soup base or stock
- 3 whole bay leaves

Preparation:

1. Heat the peanut oil in a large saucepan over medium heat.
2. Add the shallots and cook, stirring, for 3 minutes.
3. Add the rice, turmeric, coriander, cinnamon stick, salt, and cumin; and stir for 2 to 3 minutes.
4. Add the chicken soup base or stock and the bay leaves to the rice mixture, and bring to a boil.
5. Reduce the heat to low; cover and cook until the liquid is absorbed and the rice is tender—about 20 minutes. Remove from heat and let stand covered for 5 minutes.
6. Discard the cinnamon stick and bay leaves and fluff the rice with a fork, then transfer the rice to a bowl and serve immediately.

Braised Ringneck Pheasant with Cherries Jubilee

The flesh of wild ringneck pheasants can tend toward the dry side and is sometimes a bit tough. Braising is one of the best ways I've found to deal with these challenges, and a complementary sauce can enhance the flavor as the bird cooks. The Pheasant with Cherries Jubilee recipe that follows is how my mother cooked our wild birds.

Marinade Ingredients:

- ½ cup canola or sunflower oil
- ¼ cup Riesling wine
- ¼ cup pomegranate-infused balsamic vinegar
- ½ tsp. ground cloves
- ½ tsp. kosher salt
- 2 whole pheasants, cleaned and skinned

Preparation:

1. Mix the ingredients thoroughly in a small, nonreactive bowl.
2. Remove the thawed (or fresh) bird from the plastic bag and rinse it, again making sure to remove all feathers and debris, then rinse the plastic bag thoroughly.
3. Using a clean, sharp poultry needle or a knife with a thin, sharp tip, pierce the breast meat a dozen or so times, then place the bird back in the clean bag and pour the marinade over it, then roll the bird with your fingers to make sure it's thoroughly coated with the marinade. Refrigerate for at least three hours, rotating the birds a couple of times.

Sauce Ingredients:

- one 16-oz. can of sour cherries
- 2/3 cup sugar
- ¼ tsp. cloves
- 1 tsp. lemon juice
- ¼ tsp. red food color
- ¼ tsp. nutmeg
- ¼ tsp. cinnamon
- 1 tbsp. cornstarch

Preparation:

1. In a small saucepan over medium heat, heat the cherries until warm.
2. Stir in the sugar until melted.
3. Add the cornstarch to thicken, then stir in the spices.

Entrée Ingredients:

- 2 tbsp. canola or sunflower oil
- ½ cup all-purpose flour
- ½ teaspoon coarse ground black pepper
- ¼ cup reserved cherry juice
- ½ cup fat-free sour cream
- kosher salt and coarsely ground black pepper, to taste

Preparation:

1. Pre-heat the oven to 300°F.
2. In a small saucepan over medium heat, melt the butter, then stir in the cherry/ cornstarch until the entire mixture is smooth, then add the cinnamon and allspice, and stir thoroughly until bubbling gently. Remove the pan from the heat.
3. Remove the pheasant from the marinade, rinse gently, and pat dry.
4. Heat the oil in an ovenproof, 2-qt. saucepot over medium heat until shimmering.
5. Dredge the bird in the flour, salt, and pepper, and place it in the saucepan. Brown it all over—about 2 minutes per side.
6. Pour the cherry mixture over the bird, turning them if/as needed to coat it completely.
7. Place the cover on the pot and place it in the oven on the middle rack.
8. Roast for about 45 minutes, until the internal temperature reaches 1450.
9. Transfer the birds from the saucepot to a platter and cover with foil, then heat the saucepot over medium-low heat.
10. Add the water and sour cream to the saucepot and stir, removing any bits stuck to the bottom, until the liquid is fully blended and reduced by about one half.
11. Transfer the bird to a serving platter and pour the sauce into a gravy boat or serving bowl.

Glazed Baby Carrots

Ingredients:

- 1 lb. baby carrots with tops cut 1 in. from carrot then peeled
- 1/2 cup orange marmalade
- ¼ cup fresh orange juice
- 2 tbsp butter
- 1 tbsp honey mustard

Preparation:

1. Preheat the oven to 425°F.
2. In a 9 in. oven-proof pan, bring the marmalade, orange juice, butter and honey mustard to a simmer. Add the carrots, stirring to coat.
3. Transfer the pan to the oven and cook for the last 30 minutes of the pheasant's cooking time, stirring occasionally to prevent burning. Transfer to a serving dish and serve immediately.

Suggested Accompaniment

- *Pinot Noir:* Erath—Eugene, Oregon, or Bancott—Marlborough, New Zealand

Pheasant *& Cherries Jubilee over Jasmine Rice
* Squab substituted

Wonderful Whidbey

When I was growing up in Seattle, summer usually included a week with my neighbor and childhood friend, Peter, at his family's beach house near the Clinton ferry dock on Whidbey Island.

One of our sources of fun was the sawmill, about a mile up the beach from the house. There were several huge sawdust piles to slide down, and a log chute that dropped steeply from a loading platform at the top of a sheer cliff to the beach below. Although to fall off it would have meant certain injury, the chute was the only way we could get to an abandoned farm with a dilapidated chicken coop in which mice and pigeons abounded, so we braved it regularly.

We also spent a lot of our time swimming and fishing in the chilly waters of Puget Sound. Peter's family always set out several crab pots, and their favorite crab bait was freshly caught dogfish (sand sharks), so we spent many an hour fishing for dogfish from a wooden raft anchored out in front of the beach house. In the daytime, we would swim out to the raft without fear, but at night, knowing that there were dogfish prowling the inky waters beneath us, we would row a small boat out to the raft. Once on the raft, however, we all considered it great fun to push each other off; and whoa, that sure got your heart pumping!

Peter and I loved to prowl the sand- and seaweed-covered bottom at low tide, gigging spears in hand and mesh potato bags hanging from our waists, in search of flounders and sole. One morning, we donned T-shirts and beach shorts. Looking out the front window, we saw that the tide had pulled the edge of the water about as far down the beach as we'd ever seen it. Grabbing our gear, we immediately headed for the beach. Peter told me that the beach dropped off to a depth of several hundred feet about fifteen yards from where the water line now stood, and said we'd find lots of fish in the soft sands near the edge.

It didn't take long to confirm his premonition. Peter shouted with glee as two large flounder scuttled from beneath his feet, fleeing toward cover in the waving seaweed. An excellent southpaw little league pitcher, Peter deftly hurled his spear at the closest fish, pinning it to the bottom.

"Come get the other one!" he called to me as I waded toward him as he wrestled the thrashing fish into his mesh bag. I slowly approached the patch of seaweed at which he was pointing, but the fish got the jump on me, scuttling out of sight before I was close enough to throw my spear.

A short time later, walking five yards apart as we paralleled the drop off, we almost achieved a triple play. I speared a fleeing sole as Peter dipped his head below water to grab an eight-inch-wide Dungeness crab.

As he returned to the surface with his catch, however, it latched onto his right thumb with its larger claw, and Peter flung it as far as he could. So much for crab! As Peter was yowling and holding his pinched thumb, I speared a decent-sized sole fleeing from the other side of the seaweed. Two for three still wasn't bad, but now Peter was looking for something to murder!

Dungeness Crab – Photo Courtesy of Alaska Department of Fish & Wildlife

We continued up the shore, flinging our spears at fleeing fish and searching seaweed beds for more crabs, until the tide turned and began its long march back up the beach.

As we neared the sawmill, we decided to head back to the cabin, eat some breakfast, and go fishing as the tide came in.

An hour later, we swam out to the small boat tied to a buoy just beyond the edge of the drop-off, fired up the old outboard motor, and began puttering our way back up the beach toward the sawmill. We had grabbed some chips and sodas, so we were ready to be out several hours.

The tide was coming in, but we could still see the edge of the drop-off through the clear water, and we were trolling a few yards beyond it in hopes of finding salmon hunting along the edge. As Peter steered the boat out into deeper water, a fish grabbed his bait and headed away from shore. He quickly cut the engine and yanked his rod out of the pole holder. Proper etiquette required me to reel in my line, so I raised my rod and began to reel in. The extra movement was apparently a good thing, though, because another fish immediately slammed my bait.

Both Peter and I had fished for salmon quite a bit, so it didn't take us long to bring our fish into the net and drop them into the ice chest (after moving our sodas, of course!).

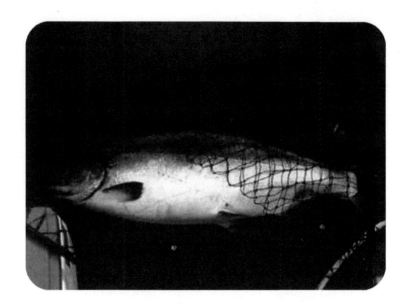

Quickly rebaiting, we trolled back through the same area, our hands clenched tightly on our rod handles. Sure enough, another salmon soon whacked my herring and headed toward deeper water. The feisty fish peeled line from my reel on energetic runs and once even leapt out of the water, but it soon tired and joined the first two bright silver fish in the ice chest.

After an hour without another bite, we decided to head in, checking the crab traps on the way. We found a couple of nice crabs in the second trap, and when we got back to the cottage, Peter's mom promised to make a Crab Louie and barbeque one of the salmon for dinner that night.

"You know what else would taste really good with a salmon?" she asked us as we cleaned the fish. "Blackberry cobbler!" she said before we could guess what she was thinking. "Why don't you boys go pick some blackberries and I'll make a cobbler for dessert?" She didn't have to ask twice!

Off again, we headed for the farm and proceeded to terrorize several mice with slingshots until we ran out of rocks. It was late afternoon by this time, so we decided to pick the blackberries and head home. We set about filling the plastic bowl we had been given with large ripe iceberg blackberries. It didn't take us long to fill the bowl with almost two quarts of the deep purple berries—not including the berries with which Peter pelted me from time to time.

The afternoon sun had dropped below the top of the cliff behind us as we climbed down the log chute—fortunately without spilling any berries or falling off.

Finally back on the sand, we trotted toward the cottage, thinking about what would surely be one of the best dinners we'd ever had. Now as I look back on that summer adventure, I'm full of happy memories of wonderful Whidbey.

AlderSmoked Coho Salmon

Ingredients:

- 1½ cup dark brown sugar, packed
- 3 tbsp. kosher salt
- 1 two to three pound coho (silver) salmon fillet, skin on, with pin bones removed and cut crosswise into 2-inch pieces
- 1 tbsp. toasted fennel seeds

Preparation:

1. Mix the brown sugar and salt together in a nonreactive bowl.
2. Working with one piece at a time, place the fillets into a glass 9×12 inch casserole dish and coat thoroughly with the sugar-salt mixture.
3. Remove the fish pieces from the pan after 16 to 20 hours and rinse under cold water to remove all of the mixture, and pat dry.
4. Light a charcoal fire of 10 to 12 briquettes in an aluminum pie plate with several small holes in the bottom. Separately, plunge about 3 cups of alter smoking chips into a bucket of water for five minutes, then remove them to a flat surface to drain and dry.
5. Place the fillets on a narrow-grooved barbeque grate sprayed with non-stick spray, and sprinkle the fennel seeds lightly over each piece.
6. Once the briquettes have a thin coating of white ash on them, spread them evenly in the pie tin using a metal poker or green stick. Place a small handful of the wood chips directly onto the hot coals, then place the grate with the fillets into the barbeque—as far away from the charcoal as possible. Close the lid on the barbeque.
7. About every 30 minutes, open the lid of the barbeque and "stir" the coals gently to allow them to get some oxygen. Add another small handful of wood chips and re-close the barbeque lid.
8. When the fish has a smoky finish and is slightly firm to the touch, remove the grate from the barbeque, then remove the fish pieces from the grate.

Caesar Salad

Ingredients:

- 1/3 cup extra virgin olive oil
- 3 tbsp. lemon juice
- 2 tsp. anchovy paste
- 1 tsp. Worcestershire sauce
- ¼ tsp. dry mustard
- 2 cloves garlic, minced
- 1 head romaine lettuce, torn or chopped into bite-sized pieces
- ½ cup grated Asiago cheese
- ½ tsp. coarsely ground black pepper
- 2 cups garlic croutons (recipe follows)

Preparation:

1. In a large wooden salad bowl, thoroughly mix the oil, lemon juice, Worcestershire sauce, mustard, and garlic.
2. Add the lettuce leaves and toss gently until they are thoroughly coated with the dressing.
3. Sprinkle the cheese and pepper over the top, add the croutons, and toss immediately before serving.

Mom's Blackberry Cobbler

Ingredients:

- ½ cup sugar
- 2 tbsp. butter, softened to room temperature
- 1 cup flour
- 1½ tsp. baking powder
- 1 cup 2% milk
- 1 pint fresh, washed and cleaned blackberries
- ¾ cup sugar
- 1 cup boiling water

Preparation:

1. Preheat the oven to 350°F.
2. In a medium bowl, mix the sugar and butter together until thoroughly blended.
3. Stir in the flour and baking soda, then add the milk, stirring constantly. Mix until creamy.
4. Pour the mixture into a 9×9-inch cake pan, then sprinkle the berries and the sugar evenly over the entire mixture.
5. Pour boiling water evenly over the mixture, then bake for 45 minutes.

Garlic Croutons

Ingredients:

- 4 large garlic cloves, peeled
- ¼ cup extra virgin olive oil
- 2 cups of ¾-inch bread cubes, cut from a loaf of Italian bread
- ½ tsp. kosher salt

Preparation:

1. Heat a large sauté pan over low heat.
2. With motor running, drop the garlic cloves through the feeder tube of a food processor or blender.
3. Scrape down the sides of the processor bowl, then start the motor again and add the oil in a slow stream through the feeder tube. Continue to puree the mixture for at least 30 seconds.
4. Strain the garlic from the oil by pressing it through a fine-mesh strainer into a nonreactive container. Reserve half of the garlic for the dressing and set aside the remaining half for another use.
5. Raise the heat under the sauté pan to medium. Place the bread cubes in a medium-sized mixing bowl and drizzle 2 tablespoons garlic oil evenly over bread, along with the salt; toss to coat.
6. Add another tablespoon of garlic oil and toss again.
7. Add the bread cubes to hot skillet and toast, turning the cubes and shaking the pan often, until the croutons are crisp and golden brown— about 5 to 7 minutes.
8. Return the croutons to the bowl and set aside to cool while preparing the salad.

CrabStuffed Flounder

Ingredients:

- four flounder fillets, 3 to 4 oz. each
- 6 oz. Dungeness crab chopped leg/claw meat
- ½ green pepper, seeds removed and diced
- ½ cup diced Walla Walla or Vidalia sweet onion
- 2 tbsp. diced celery
- 1½ cups crushed saltine crackers
- ½ tsp. kosher salt
- 1 tsp. coarsely ground black pepper
- 2 large eggs
- 1 cup mayonnaise
- 5 tbsp. Worcestershire sauce
- 5 tbsp. Dijon mustard
- 2 tbsp. lemon juice
- 2 tbsp. freshly grated parmesan cheese

Preparation:

1. Preheat the oven to 350°F, and spray a small casserole dish with non-stick cooking spray.
2. In a medium-sized, nonreactive bowl, combine the crabmeat, green pepper, onion, celery, crushed crackers, salt, and pepper; and mix thoroughly.
3. In a separate bowl, combine the eggs, mayonnaise, and Worcestershire sauce, mustard, and lemon juice; and mix thoroughly.
4. Pour the egg mixture into the crabmeat mixture and mix thoroughly.
5. Spoon the crabmeat mixture evenly onto each fillet, then roll each fillet from the tail forward. Secure each roll with one or two toothpicks, then place each roll into the casserole dish. Sprinkle each roll lightly with grated cheese.
6. Bake, uncovered, for 25 minutes or until the fish flakes easily when tested with a fork.

* Grouper, "Swai," and orange roughly are good alternatives.

Green Beans with Bacon and Pecans

Ingredients:

- 1 pound fresh green or pole beans, washed and drained
- 4 slices smoked bacon, coarsely chopped
- ½ cup (about 2 medium) shallots, diced
- 2 tbsp. walnut oil
- 2 tsp. lemon balsamic vinegar
- ½ tsp. kosher salt
- ¼ cup pecans, toasted and coarsely chopped
- 1 tbsp. fresh basil leaves, chopped

Preparation:

1. Preheat the oven to 350°F.
2. Spread the pecans on a cookie sheet and cook for 10 minutes. Transfer the pecans to a cutting board and chop coarsely.
3. Boil 2 cups water in a 2-quart saucepot with a steamer insert. Place the beans into the steamer insert, cover, and cook until crisp-tender—about 8 to 10 minutes.
4. While the beans are steaming, cook the bacon in a large sauté pan until it is crisp and remove to a paper towel-covered plate to drain.
5. Place the shallots into a large serving bowl, and crumble the bacon over the shallots and mix thoroughly.
6. Transfer the steamed beans to the pan with the bacon fat and cook for 2 minutes on medium heat.
7. Transfer the cooked beans to the bowl with the shallots and bacon, then add the oil, vinegar, and salt; and toss to mix thoroughly.
8. Sprinkle the pecans and the basil leaves over the mixture, gently toss, and serve.

Suggested Accompaniment

- *Pinot Grigio (Pinot Gris):* Placido—Tuscany, Italy, or King Estate—Willamette Valley, Oregon

Crab-Stuffed Flounder

Bagging the Wiley Walnut

My family pursued a wide spectrum of fish and game in Washington State in the 1960s and '70s, and on one occasion, Dad and I returned home from one of our outings with a very unique harvest.

It was mid-October, and Dad was eager to head over the Cascade Mountains. We usually started the season, hunting pheasants at a farm owned by our friends, the Bensons, but Dad had a different plan in mind. "Let's go down to Yakima," he said as he arrived home from work the day before we would depart. "Remember that farm with all those quail we hunted last season?"

"Yeah," I responded. "That was a blast—even though I didn't hit very many!"

"Well, you've been practicing a lot since then, so I'll bet you'll do better this year," he said with encouragement.

Yakima was a three-hour drive from our home in south Seattle, so we hit the road early on Saturday morning. Shortly before noon, we pulled into a long drive onto the farm we wanted to hunt.

"You probably don't remember us," Dad said when the farmer opened the door, "but my son and I hunted your farm last November."

"Sure, I remember you!" the friendly fellow replied. "You had quite a time chasing quail, as I recall."

"You do remember!" Dad replied. "If there aren't any other hunters already out on your property, we'd sure appreciate it if we could chase them again."

"There aren't any other hunters, so go ahead. Just remember to close the gates behind you coming or going."

"Will do!" Dad answered, smiling. They shook hands, and we turned to go back to the car when the farmer spoke again.

"By the way," he said, "if you find anything in the fields—green peppers, cantaloupes, watermelons, and the like—feel free to take whatever you want. We finished picking a couple of weeks ago, but there are a few leftovers that weren't ripe then. Oh, and there are some broken wooden crates at the end of the road by the canal that you can use to carry whatever you find."

"Thank you—again!" Dad answered. By the time we reached the end of the canal road and ate a quick sandwich, we heard the "*pop pop pop*" of shotguns in the distance.

"I guess that's our cue!" Dad said, shutting the car door and handing me my shotgun. I already had on my vest—loaded with shells—and was eager to get started. Penny, our white-and-liver spotted German Shorthaired Pointer, was also ready and had headed up the side of the road by the time Dad and I started walking.

"Penny! Here!" She raced back to us without delay, then charged into the brush and vines next to the canal. Dad crossed to the other side of the ditch to have a shot if the birds flew that way. By mid-October, the canal's flow had been reduced to a shallow trickle, but it still provided moisture for foliage and wildlife, including quail, pheasants, and rabbits.

With Penny sweeping back and forth in front of us to catch the scent of a bird, we made our way slowly toward the end of the canal a half-mile away. Her stubby tail began to vibrate, signaling that she had found scent. A second later, she locked on point, her eyes peering intently into a small cluster of brush and vines. As I came up behind her, I could see Dad coming up on my left with his gun ready. "Whoa," I said gently to Penny to steady her.

When Dad was set, I stepped forward past Penny, still locked on point, and kicked the weeds to flush the bird or birds. Several quail burst simultaneously from the grass, darting and weaving as they flew. Two flew to my right, while the other three veered left, heading up the canal for cover. I took careful aim at one of the birds and pulled the trigger.

Boom! The bird fell just as Dad shot, and his bird fell as I took aim at my second bird. By this time, though, it had veered into thick cover. *Boom!* Dad fired a second shot from his 20-gauge shotgun.

Penny retrieved Dad's two birds, and my bird had fallen in the open less than forty yards from where I had been standing, so I was able to pick it up without having to call her over to me.

Within a few minutes, we were under way again, walking slowly to where the other birds had landed. As we approached, we could hear a number of quail "chittering" back and forth nervously.

Valley Quail – Photo courtesy of OR Dept of Fish & Wildlife

Penny soon locked on point again. I raised my gun in preparation for a shot as I stepped toward her. *Whirrrrrrr!* One of the little missiles launched itself inches from Penny's nose. Although a flushing bird always makes me jump a little, I was ready, and quickly lined up the shot and dropped the bird. Penny had barely moved from where she had pointed the first bird when she locked on point again.

Dad was ready as the second bird burst from cover and veered hard to head back down the canal in the opposite direction. Not fooled, Dad lined it up quickly and made a great shot.

We both quickly reloaded our guns as Penny tore after Dad's bird. When she returned, we continued toward the brush pile and the rest of the covey. Penny did her best to point and hold the birds, but they were already on edge and began flushing, one and two at a time, at random. By the time the shooting stopped, we had five more birds on the ground for a total of ten birds—in less than an hour!

As I turned back toward the car at the end of the canal road, Dad noticed that the ground at the base of several tall trees was covered with hard, black husks. Picking one up, Dad reached into his pocket, pulled out his pocketknife, and pried the husk open to find a tasty walnut inside.

We then noticed, tossed haphazardly in the brush near the trees, a dozen or so wooden crates. Some were nearly unusable, while others had only minor cracks and broken slats.

"Now that we know where the crates are, and that there are walnuts here too, let's go find some more birds and come back later." Off we went up a shallow ravine toward the top of a small hillside. Along the top, we could see rows of short posts holding vines on stout wire. Concord grapes! Although most of the crop had been harvested, there were still a few small clusters of bright purple grapes.

We hunted the edge of the vines but didn't find any quail. As we approached the opposite end of the hill, though, Dad spotted some mourning doves flying our way. He called Penny to his side and motioned me to kneel down.

Pass shooting has never been my forte, but I took two shots and missed them both while Dad dropped both birds at which he shot. "They're flying down-wind, so you have to lead them quite a bit!" he said.

Ten minutes and three groups of doves later, we had six birds on the ground.

Mourning Dove – Photo courtesy of Texas Parks & Wildlife

As we picked up the birds, Dad said, "Ten quail, six doves, all the walnuts we can carry, and Concord grapes—not a bad day!"

As we traversed across a couple of fields on our way back down the hill to the car, however, we came upon the green peppers, cantaloupes, and watermelons the farmer had mentioned. Some were still in good shape, so we filled our game vests with as much as we could carry and decided to come back for more once we got a few crates.

By the end of the day, Dad had decided that we head home with our bounty rather than staying the night. Where would we sleep, after all, with the back end of the station wagon filled with two crates each of green and red peppers, cantaloupes and watermelons, plus a crate of Concord grapes and about twenty pounds of walnuts— oh, and our birds? We couldn't forget about the birds!

Melted Brie with Chopped Walnuts

Ingredients:

- 1 8 oz. wheel of brie cheese
- ¼ cup black walnuts, toasted and coarsely chopped
- water crackers
- 1 bunch ripe Concord or red seedless grapes

Preparation:

1. Score the top of the cheese wheel with a large *X*, place it on a microwave-proof plate and heat it for 25 to 35 seconds—or until the cheese starts to melt.
2. Remove the plate from the microwave and sprinkle the cheese with the walnut pieces.
3. Surround the cheese with the crackers, garnish with the grape bunch, and serve.

Creamy Fennel Slaw

Ingredients:

- 2 large fennel bulbs, cored and coarsely chopped
- 1 carrot, grated
- 1 sweet onion, minced
- 3 green onions, minced
- 1 cup reduced-fat mayonnaise
- 1 cup buttermilk
- 2 tbsp. white wine vinegar
- 2 tbsp. stone-ground mustard
- ½ cup white sugar
- 1 pinch cayenne pepper
- 1 tsp. kosher salt, divided
- 1 clove garlic, minced

Preparation:

1. In a large bowl, mix the fennel, carrot, sweet onion, and green onions.
2. In a separate bowl, blend the mayonnaise, buttermilk, vinegar, mustard, sugar, cayenne pepper, and 3/4 teaspoon of the salt. Mash the remaining salt and the garlic together, then whisk them the dressing.
3. Pour the dressing evenly over the fennel mixture, tossing to coat. Cover and refrigerate 6 to 8 hours, or overnight, before serving.

DoveandQuail Ragout

Ingredients:

- 3 tbsp. extra virgin olive oil
- 2 large cloves garlic, diced
- 4 cleaned and skinned quail, deboned and with all shotgun pellets removed, then diced into ½-inch cubes
- cleaned and skinned doves, deboned and with all shotgun pellets removed, then diced into ½-inch cubes
- ½ cup Walla Walla onions, thinly sliced vertically
- ½ cup green and/or red peppers, coarsely chopped
- 2 cups Yukon Gold potatoes, cut into ½ cubes
- 14–16 oz. can of quartered baby artichoke hearts, drained
- 3–4 tbsp. all-purpose flour
- 1 cup chicken soup base or stock
- kosher salt and coarsely ground black pepper, to taste

Preparation:

1. In a large sauté pan over medium heat, sauté the garlic until it releases its fragrance, then add the bird meat and cook until just browned.
2. Add the next 4 ingredients and sauté until they begin to soften.
3. Sprinkle the flour over the mixture, stirring to evenly coat the ingredients.
4. Slowly add the soup base or stock, stirring.
5. Reduce the heat to medium low, season the mixture with salt and pepper, then cover and simmer until the potatoes are cooked through—about 20 to 25 minutes—stirring occasionally.
6. Transfer the mixture to a serving bowl and serve immediately

Fried Sweet Corn

Ingredients:

- 2 tbsp. extra virgin olive oil
- 4 husked and rinsed ears of fresh sweet corn, kernels sliced from cob
- 1 red bell pepper, diced
- kosher salt and coarsely ground black pepper, to taste

Preparation:

1. Heat the oil over medium-high heat in a large, heavy bottomed sauté pan.
2. Add the cayenne pepper, corn, and red peppers.
3. Stir occasionally, adding salt and black pepper to taste for 10 minutes or until entire mixture is heated through.
4. Transfer to a large bowl and serve.

Suggested Accompaniment

- *Riesling:* Covey Run—Columbia Valley, Washington, or Penfold's Thomas Hyland—South Australia

Dove-and-Quail Ragout

Skagit River Steelhead

The Skagit River, in northwestern Washington, flows from Sullivan Lake, a large reservoir in the Cascade Mountains, to Puget Sound. In western Washington's wet winters, and continuing through the spring snowmelt runoff, the Skagit can be a roiling, dangerous morass that can only be fished by boat.

When the weather clears and the spring runoff has abated, however, the Skagit becomes a navigable highway for a number of ocean-going fish as they head upstream to spawn. Runs of spring chinook, coho, and, on alternating years, pink salmon, along with their cousins, steelhead trout, move up the river to their birthplaces to continue the circle of life. Too, ospreys, bald eagles, crows and ravens, and various other predatory or carrion-eating birds, along with rainbow and Dolly Varden trout, wait to feast on each run.

A strong run of steelhead in September 1974 encouraged my father, my college friend, Rich, and I to head toward the town of Concrete, Washington, which sat on the banks of the Skagit River about ten miles from the Sullivan Lake hydroelectric dam. Although none of us had ever fished the Skagit, Dad had talked with some of his friends who had, so he had a good idea of where we should go. We brought a full spectrum of rods, streamer flies, and lures as well as a container of salt-cured salmon egg clusters.

We parked at a shaded pull-off that provided well-used trails down a short bank to the river's edge. From there, Dad headed upstream while Rich and I moved downstream toward a large pool.

Wasting no time, Dad's line was in the water first; and less than five minutes later, we heard him yell, "Fish on!" Drifting an egg cluster past a large rock into the eddies below it, he had hooked a nice steelhead and played it expertly as it skittered through the crystal-clear water. After a short fight, the fish lost the battle and was quickly dropped into an Igloo ice chest.

"So much for the 'first fish' bet!" Rich said, smiling, as he crawled over a fallen log.

"Yeah," I replied, "but maybe it won't take 'biggest fish'!"

After clearing the log, I picked out a spot that was shallow for about fifteen feet into the river while Rich continued down the river's edge, stopping nearly fifty yards downstream. We each quickly selected a lure and began casting.

As I retrieved my second cast, a large shadow swung out from behind a rock no more than five or six feet from where I was standing in ankle-deep water. Stealthily, the shadow moved toward my bait as it bounced along the bottom then inhaled the egg mass. I released the bail on my spinning reel and allowed the fish to swim slowly away until it was about thirty feet out into the river's current. Gently but firmly, I raised the rod tip and gave it a quick tug. "Fish on!" I shouted as the water exploded around the now-surging fish.

Although I hadn't gotten a real good look at it, I was pretty sure that the fish was a steelhead in the ten-pound neighborhood. I was using fifteen-pound test monofilament with an eight-pound test leader, so I would need to be careful not to "horse" the fish too much—especially in this log-strewn stretch of river.

The reel sang as the fish took off downstream. I knew I had plenty of line, but it soon became clear that the fish was headed for a short drop-off, below which were some rapids. Keeping the rod tip as high as I could, I gently tightened the drag to put more pressure on the fish. It worked, and I was able to turn the fish back toward me. A little at a time, I took back line, also trying to lead the fish toward shallow water. At first, it fought to stay in the deeper water; but it eventually succumbed to the pressure, and I was able to swing the fish toward a shallow pool.

By this time, Rich had come back upstream toward me. He waded into the pool about fifteen or twenty feet below the fish, moving to the river side of the pool to cut off any escape attempts. Fortunately, though, the fish had tired enough that I was able to "beach" him in the shallow water and soft sand.

He was a beautiful hook-nosed "buck" steelhead that later weighed in at nine pounds ten ounces. "Beat that!" I teased Rich as he admired the fish. "I'll try, but that's a heck of a fish!" he replied.

It was Rich's turn. Within about ten minutes, he hooked a bright "hen" steelhead that danced across the surface of the water in the middle of the river. Rich waded carefully out into the roiling water until he reached thigh depth. Steadying his balance, he steered the fish away from several large rocks and fallen tree limbs until it tired enough to let him lead it into shallow water and land it.

At about three o'clock, I heard Dad shout, "We aren't the only ones fishing! See the bald eagles?" he asked as he pointed to a large, craggy branch hanging out over the river further upstream.

"I see them," I answered. Just then, one of the huge birds launched itself from its perch and, swooping toward shallow water along the far bank, reached into the water and locked its talons on a fish we later guessed to be nearly five pounds. Flapping steadily to gain altitude, the bird flew to a nearby treetop where a small eaglet was waiting, barely visible. As the nestling watched, the adult proceeded to rip the fish into small strips, which the smaller bird gobbled up quickly.

We were nearing the end of a perfect day of fishing, and as the sun began its slow plunge toward the western horizon, I decided to make one last cast with a bright pink egg-imitator "fly." On the retrieve, I hooked a feisty twenty-three-inch Dolly Varden. Although it was fair game, I decided not to keep the chunky fish. It was my first Dolly, and I was glad just to have had the chance to catch one.

Dolly Varden – Photo courtesy of Alaska Department of Fish & Game

Remembering that we still had a long drive facing into the late afternoon sun ahead of us, we packed up our gear and headed for the car. In a little over four hours, we had managed to catch five steelhead between us as well as a couple of small rainbow trout and the Dolly Varden. Not bad for our first-ever visit to the Skagit!

Peppery Deviled Eggs with Chives and Caviar

Ingredients:

- 6 hardboiled eggs, cooled and peeled, then rinsed and patted dry, and halved lengthwise
- 2½ tsp. pepper mélange (pink, white, black, and green peppercorns)
- ½ tsp. of the liquid from a jar of stuffed green olives
- ¼ cup reduced-fat mayonnaise
- 1 tsp. Dijon mustard
- ¼ tsp. grey sea salt
- ¼ tsp. sugar
- 1 tbsp. chives, cut into ½-inch pieces
- 3 tsp. of black or red caviar, chilled, divided

Preparation:

1. Combine the ground pepper, olive liquid, mayonnaise, mustard, salt, and sugar with the egg yolks. Using a fork, stir to mash and thoroughly combine the ingredients.
2. Place the mixture into a small plastic bag and cut a small hole at one of the corners. Arrange the egg white halves on an egg dish and squeeze the mixture into each of the halves.
3. Chill for at least 1 hour in the refrigerator before serving, then sprinkle some chives over each egg half, and top each egg half with a small dollop (about 1/8 tsp.) of the caviar.

Strawberry Shortcake

Ingredients:

- 3 cups all-purpose flour
- ¼ cup white sugar
- 4 tsp. baking powder
- ¾ tsp. cream of tartar
- 1 cup butter, softened
- 2/3 cup Half-and-Half
- 1 egg, beaten
- 4 cups fresh strawberries, washed, stems removed, and cut into thin slices
- 4 tbsp. white sugar

Preparation:

1. Preheat the oven to 350°F.
2. In a large mixing bowl, stir together the flour, sugar, baking powder and cream of tartar. Cut in the butter with a pastry blender or two knives, then stir in the Half-and-Half and egg.
3. Transfer the dough to a lightly floured surface and knead for 2 to 3 minutes, then press into a half-inch thick sheet. Cut into 2-inch squares and transfer the squares to a baking sheet.
4. Bake for 20 minutes, or until golden, then remove to a cooling rack.
5. Sprinkle the sugar over the sliced berries in a medium bowl and toss.
6. When the shortcakes have cooled to room temperature, split each cake across the middle, place in individual serving bowls, fill with sugared berries, and top with whipped cream or Half-and-Half.

Steelhead Gravlax and Spring Greens Salad with Oriental Dressing

Ingredients:

- 2 1½ to 2 lb. descaled steelhead fillets
- 3 tbsp. kosher salt
- 2 tbsp. sugar
- 1 tsp. freshly ground black pepper
- 1 good-size bunch dill, roughly chopped, stems and all
- ½ cup dry gin

Preparation:

1. Lay both fillets, skin side down, on a plastic wrap-covered platter. Sprinkle with the salt, sugar, and pepper, spread the dill over them, and splash on the gin. Sandwich the fillets together, tail to tail, then wrap tightly in plastic wrap. Cover the sandwich with another platter and something that weighs about a pound, an unopened can of coffee or beans, for example. Refrigerate.
2. Open the package every 12 to 24 hours and baste inside and out with the accumulated juices.
3. On the second or third day, when the flesh has lost its translucence, slice thinly on the bias and without the skin. Serve with rye bread, or pumpernickel, and lemon wedges.

Salad Ingredients:

- 4 cups fresh, mixed garden greens (watercress, endive, baby bib, and baby spinach leaves)
- 2 tbsp. roasted walnuts, coarsely chopped
- 1/8 cup oriental salad dressing (see page 17)
- Gravlax, cut across the grain into 16 thin slices
- 1 tsp. fennel seeds, divided (optional)

Preparation:

1. Toss the salad greens, walnuts, and oriental dressing together in a medium mixing bowl.
2. Spoon out 1 cup of the mixture onto each of 4 chilled salad plates.
3. Arrange the Gravlax slices on top of each salad, sprinkle with ¼ teaspoon fennel seeds, and serve.

* Store-bought, farm-raised salmons or steelheads are acceptable substitutes.

Soft Breadsticks

Ingredients:

- 2 tbsp. granulated sugar
- ¾ tsp. active dry yeast
- 1 cup plus 1 tbsp. warm water
- 3 cups bread flour
- 1½ tsp. salt
- ¼ cup butter, softened, plus 2 tbsp., melted
- ½ tsp. granulated garlic

Preparation:

1. Dissolve the sugar and yeast in the warm water in a small bowl and let the mixture sit for 5 minutes or until it begins to foam.
2. Combine the flour and salt in a large bowl. Mix the softened butter into the flour with a mixing spoon.
3. When the yeast mixture is foamy, pour it into the flour mixture and knead the dough for 10 minutes.
4. Place the dough in a covered container and let it sit until it doubles in size— about 90 minutes.
5. When the dough has doubled, measure out portions about the size of a golf ball and roll the dough between your hands or on a lightly floured countertop to form 7-inch-long sticks.
6. Place the dough on parchment paperlined baking sheets, cover and set aside until the dough doubles in size again— about 90 minutes.
7. Preheat the oven to 400°F.
8. Bake the breadsticks for 12 minutes, or until golden brown.
9. When the breadsticks come out of the oven, immediately brush each one with melted butter and sprinkle with a little granulated garlic.

Suggested Accompaniment

- *Chardonnay:* Greg Norman (Australian) or Kendall Jackson—Central Coast, California, or Covey Run—Columbia Valley, Washington

Steelhead Gravlax on Toasts

Partridges Aplenty

Washington State University (WSU), located in Pullman, Washington, is about six hours' drive east of Seattle. The farmland just south of Pullman is surrounded by open, rolling wheat fields and bordered to the east by deep, gnarly ravines. Lots of upland game birds, including red-legged partridge (also known as chukar or chukar partridge), Hungarian partridge (also known as gray partridge or Huns), and ringneck pheasant thrive in the area.

Early in October 1976, my dad invited me to join him and my brother, Mitch, for a chukar hunt in Pullman. That weekend was WSU's homecoming weekend, which happened to fall on the same day as the upland bird hunting season opener, so he figured that we could do some bird hunting before catching the football game on Saturday night.

We arrived in Pullman after stopping only once for gas and to let Josh, Dad's German Shorthaired Pointer, stretch his legs and water a bush. When we arrived at Mitch's dormitory complex, Dad went inside to find Mitch and meet his roommates. They soon returned with one of the roommates, Fritz. Fritz told us that he lived in the nearby farming community of Washtucna, was a bird hunter, and knew the area we would be hunting the next day; so we were more than happy to have him join us for the hunt.

The next morning, we loaded our gear into the car and headed out. Six or seven miles south of Colton, Fritz directed us down a dirt access road that led quickly around the end of a small knob.

As we came to a stop, Fritz explained his game plan. "Just beyond that knob is the top end of a long ravine that opens up into a canyon. The top end of the ravine is brushy, and there are usually

Huns along the edge of the wheat field. As the ravine opens up and begins to fall away, we can go left or right and hunt along the top edge of the canyon. We'll find both Huns and chukar—and maybe a pheasant or two!"

Josh didn't really care about Fritz's plan and had already charged off into the heavy cover fifty yards up the road from us. Before we had finished tying our bootlaces and donning our hunting vests, he was locked on point.

As we hurried to catch up to the dog, Mitch saw movement in the grass. "It looks like Huns," he said. "We need to spread out a little."

Dad moved in directly behind Josh while I stepped a few yards to the right of the dog, and Mitch angled further up the hill to my right. Fritz dropped down into the brush to the left, so we had the birds flanked.

"Whoa!" Dad said to Josh, who had been holding his point for several minutes. As he stepped forward, kicking the grass in front of the dog, a covey of seven birds exploded from the ankle-deep grass. Four veered to the right, two veered left toward Fritz, and one flew straight away. Mitch was lightning fast with his Ithaca 20-gauge pump and quickly had two birds on the ground. I shot each barrel of my 12-gauge Browning side-by-side in rapid succession, knocking one bird to the ground and clipping the other. Dad, having already dropped his single, saw my second bird teeter and finished it off with his 20-gauge over-under. Not to be outdone, Fritz dispatched his two birds with his 20-gauge Remington pump.

"So is it going to be like this all afternoon?" Mitch asked Fritz as Josh retrieved the birds.

"We might have just shot all the birds we'll see today, but I don't think that'll be the case!" Fritz said, laughing.

We continued down the draw, with several birds flushing wild far in front of us. As we neared the end of the field, the brush became very thick, and Josh's short tail began to twitch. We knew that this kind of cover could be hiding just about anything—Huns, chukar, or pheasant. Everyone readied their guns as we watched Josh creep stealthily through the heavy cover, finally locking on point.

Whirrrrrrrr! A huge rooster pheasant blasted out of a clump of Indian tobacco between Mitch and me. As we both swung to line up on it, we heard more *"whirrrrr"* sounds as another rooster and four Huns exploded from the grass in front of Josh and Dad. Dad turned to take aim at one of the Huns, and when I saw that Fritz was already swinging on the Huns veering his direction, I lined up on the second rooster. In a matter of seconds, we had four more Huns and both pheasants on the ground.

After collecting the birds, we stopped to rest and fixed sandwiches of mayonnaise, beefsteak, tomatoes, and Cougar Gold sharp cheddar cheese made at the WSU Agriculture Department's dairy. Reenergized, we were soon ready to go again.

Mitch walked along the edge of the wheat field while Fritz, Dad, and I dropped below the edge of the plateau. As we came upon a shallow ridge dividing two small ravines, a huge whitetail buck erupted from out of the shade of a sumac tree and bounded out of sight. I wasn't a deer hunter at that point in my life, but the sight of that beautiful buck sure got my juices flowing!

We were concerned that the bounding deer would make any birds in the area nervous, so we stopped for a few minutes to let things settle down. Apparently, our strategy worked because as we crested the next small ridge, Josh locked on point again. This time, however, there was very little vegetation in which any birds could hide, so we were skeptical. Dad wasn't and said, as we moved slowly forward, "If you hire a consultant, you better follow his advice!" The breeze was blowing steadily across the hillside directly into our faces, and we realized that Josh had picked up the birds' scent from almost sixty yards away!

As Fritz had predicted, these birds were chukars, which are prone to flushing one, two, or three at a time, and in different directions. They did just that, and we each had several shot opportunities. When the smoke cleared, we had five of the handsome birds in hand.

We continued across the hillside until we reached the far end of the field and could see the tops of telephone poles next to the highway almost a mile to the west.

"That sure looks like a long way back to the car!" Dad said tiredly.

Laughing, Fritz suggested that we just start walking because we'd probably get depressed if we knew how far it actually was. But we had far too much fun that afternoon to get depressed about anything because there were partridges aplenty!

Basil Leaves with Goat Cheese and Kalamata Olives

Ingredients:

- 18 to 20 large basil leaves, washed and patted dry
- goat cheese, sliced into 18 to 20 thin (1/8-inch) discs
- 9 to 10 Kalamata olives, pitted and halved

Preparation:

1. Evenly space the basil leaves on a serving platter.
2. Position one cheese disc on each basil leaf, then place one olive half on each cheese disc.
3. Chill and serve.

Chilled Green Bean Salad with Walnuts and Crumbled Bleu Cheese

Ingredients:

- 1 cup walnuts, toasted and coarsely chopped
- ¾ cup extra virgin olive oil
- ¼ cup lemon balsamic vinegar
- 2 tsp. dried and crumbled dill
- 1 tsp. minced garlic
- ¼ tsp. kosher salt
- ½ tsp. coarsely ground black pepper
- 4 cups (1½ lb.) fresh green beans, washed and trimmed, with strings removed and cut into 1 to 1½-inch pieces
- 2 cups water
- 1 small Walla Walla or Vidalia (sweet) onion, coarsely chopped
- 4 oz. crumbled Bleu cheese

Preparation:

1. Preheat oven to 350°F.
2. Place walnuts in a shallow, ovenproof pan and bake for 8 to 10 minutes; remove and set aside to cool.
3. In a small mixing bowl, combine and thoroughly mix the oil, vinegar, dill, garlic, salt, and pepper; cover and refrigerate.
4. Place the beans in a steamer basket, boil the water and steam the beans for 15 minutes or until they are just tender. Remove from the heat and immediately plunge them into a bowl of cold water, then drain and pat dry.
5. In a large bowl, combine the beans, walnuts, onion, and cheese and toss well, then cover and refrigerate.
6. Twenty to thirty minutes before serving, pour the dressing over the bean mixture, then toss immediately before serving.

Partridges in Blueberry Sauce

Dressing/Marinade Ingredients:

- ½ cup of blueberry sauce (see below)
- 2 tbsp. balsamic vinegar
- 2 tbsp. soy sauce
- 2 tsp. Dijon mustard
- 1 tbsp. fresh ginger root (peeled, then finely grated)
- 2 garlic cloves, peeled and mashed
- ½ tsp. Kosher salt
- ½ tsp. chili powder
- ½ tsp. freshly ground black pepper, or to taste
- 2/3 cup extra-virgin olive oil

Preparation:

1. Whisk the ingredients together and use half for the marinade, and the other half for the salad dressing you'll use as you serve. This can be made, and kept refrigerated, a day or two ahead of time.

Blueberry Sauce Ingredients:

- 2 pints of fresh blueberries—rinsed, drained, and picked over
- 1 cup of powdered sugar
- ¼ cup Triple Sec, or a similar liquor

Preparation:

1. In a saucepan, cook the blueberries, powdered sugar, and liqueur over medium- to medium-high heat until the berries are quite broken down. Cool and break them down further in the food processor.

Entrée Ingredients:

- 4 cleaned and skinned chukar or Hungarian partridges
- ½ cup chicken stock or soup base
- 1 pound of fresh spinach—washed and picked over to remove unwanted pieces and stems
- 4 plum tomatoes cut into ¼-inch slices
- 2/3 cup of fresh whole blueberries, washed and picked over
- 2 scallions, finely chopped

Preparation:

1. Preheat the oven to 400°F.
2. Lightly coat a small casserole dish with cooking spray.
3. Remove the partridges from the marinade and rinse with cold water. Pat dry and place in the casserole dish.
4. Add the stock or soup base, cover the birds loosely with aluminum foil, and bake for 20 to 25 minutes until the juices run clear.
5. Toss the spinach, scallions, and toasted walnuts with enough dressing to coat. Place a serving on each plate and arrange the remaining ingredients for presentation. Drizzle the salad with a touch of the blueberry sauce and put the rest of the sauce in a serving container for the table.
6. Place a bird on or next to each salad and serve immediately.

Rice Pilaf with Mushrooms and Walnuts

Ingredients:

- ¼ cup butter
- ½ cup uncooked medium-grain rice
- ¼ cup uncooked orzo pasta
- 1 cup fresh shiitake or baby portabella mushrooms, stems removed and cut into ¼-inch slices
- ½ cup yellow onion, chopped
- ¼ cup celery, minced
- 2 cups chicken soup base or broth
- 2 tbsp. fresh parsley, chopped
- ¼ tsp. dried marjoram
- ¼ tsp. ground black pepper
- ½ cup toasted walnuts, chopped

Preparation:

1. Melt the butter in a large, heavy-bottomed skillet over medium-low heat. Add the rice, orzo, mushrooms, onion, and celery. Stir constantly until the rice is lightly browned.
2. Mix in the remaining ingredients and bring to a boil, then reduce heat to low, cover, and allow to simmer until the rice is tender—about 18 to 20 minutes. Remove from heat and let stand 10 minutes before serving.

Suggested Accompaniment

- *Fume Blanc:* Barnard Griffin—Columbia Valley, Washington, or Chateau St. Jean—Sonoma Valley, California

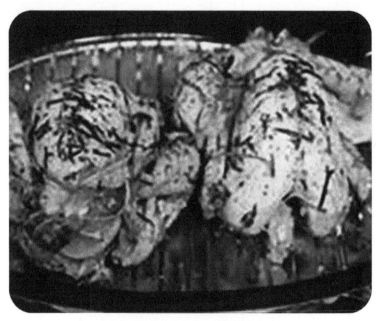

Roast Partridges* with Blueberry Sauce
* Cornish Hens substituted

A Mixed Bag

The fall of 1983 was a time of transition. My wife and I had a one-year-old son who had begun to walk and talk. I was entering into a new phase of my career with The Boeing Company in Seattle, Washington; and a colleague at work, Randy, had convinced me to join him on my first big-game hunt. As I'll explain later, it turned out to be a bit of a transition for Randy as well!

Randy always hunted ducks with his brother on opening weekend—mid-October in Washington. We met in the town of Vantage, on the western bank of the Columbia River, at noon on Sunday, then headed north to Banks Lake to hunt mule deer along the high cliffs on the west side of the lake. The weather was clear and mild, and our hopes were high as we drove northward.

Leaving the main highway between Ephrata and Soap Lake, we paralleled the west side of Banks Lake and crossed vast expanses of wheat fields, sage brush, and basalt rock formations. I knew that there were lots of mule deer in the area—including some trophy-sized animals.

It was almost four o'clock as we rounded a long bend in the road to find a harvested wheat field in which we could see hundreds of geese near the farthest corner. Because we had to sneak up on the geese, Randy's black lab, Badger, would have to stay in the truck. There was a rise between us and the geese, so once we snuck down the bank from the road into the grass, we were able to move easily and quickly for most of the way. As we neared the top of the rise, however, we had to drop to our hands and knees, and crawl slowly into the foot-high wheat stubble. Moving slowly, we crawled for a little over a hundred yards. At this point, the geese would be able to see us if we stayed on our hands and knees, so we dropped our bellies and crawled, commando style.

One thing I quickly realized was that my 12-gauge side-by-side would limit the number of shots I could take. Randy had a 12-gauge pump and would have one more shot than I would—at least for the initial barrage.

As we closed to forty yards, Randy whispered, "Pick out a couple of birds standing next to each other and take them first. Then, when the flock gets up, pick a bird you can take cleanly." I nodded in response.

"On my mark," he hissed as he lined up his first shot. "Now!"

Almost simultaneously, I heard his gun roar and saw a large goose drop. I had targeted a pair of sentry birds and pulled the trigger. Both birds crumpled at once, and within seconds, a swirling, honking cloud of frightened geese filled the air. We both rose to our knees, and Randy's second shot thundered, dropping another honker. I zeroed in on a bird angling to my right and sighed with relief when it crashed into the wheat stubble. To my left, I heard Randy's third shot and his whoop of joy as another bird bit the dust.

We had both managed to kill our limits, so we just sat back and watched as nearly a thousand geese rose into the sky and headed for Banks Lake to the east. We retrieved our game and headed back to the truck, realizing that the field had been filled with a massive throng of geese and was now empty of everything but Randy and me, and our six birds.

We rose the next morning before dawn and headed toward a large brush-and-tree-filled canyon in which my dad and I found several coveys of quail the year before. At the foot of the canyon, which opened onto a sandy cove of Banks Lake, a power line access road led upward across the steep south side of the canyon for nearly a mile until it reached the rocky top of the ridge.

Because we expected to run into both deer and birds, I carried my shotgun while Randy had his 7-mm rifle with a 3×9 scope. Badger came along but stayed close to Randy as we edged our way up the rocky trail.

As we neared the top, I pointed to a couple of large pine trees and said, "Once we pass those trees, the road will double back to the left, and we'll be at the top of the ridge. At that point, we need to be side-by-side because anything can happen!"

Moments later, it did! As Badger loped out ahead, a fork-horn mule deer exploded out of cover to Randy's right in a stiff, four-legged bounce. As it raced away from us, a small flock of chukar exploded from the cheat grass to my left. I was more interested in the deer and watched as Randy tried to put the crosshairs on the bouncing target. Sixty or seventy yards out, the deer stopped and turned to look at us, and Randy dropped it with a single shot.

"I've never seen a deer hop like that!" he yelled.

"That's the way mule deer usually run, especially when they're trying to cover a lot of ground quickly. It's called stotting." I replied.

"Black-tails don't do that!"

"Of course, they don't. They'd trip and fall in the thick underbrush!"

We gave the deer several minutes before walking to it. On the way, he chambered a second round just in case the deer wasn't finished. It was dead, but as we knelt beside it, another fork-horn bolted from behind a sage bush patch and crossed directly in front of us. This deer "stotted" too, and I nearly laughed as I watched Randy try to put the scope's crosshairs on its chest.

He finally shot, and the deer stumbled but didn't go down. By the time he had chambered another round, the deer had plunged over the edge of the hill into the deep canyon.

I quickly field dressed the first deer while Randy and Badger went to look for the second animal. By the time they returned, I had the deer tied to my pack frame, and we headed toward the truck.

About a third of the way down the road, Badger dashed off ahead of us, clearly excited. "What is that?" I asked Randy as we saw a large "lump" in the road, about fifty yards ahead.

"That, my friend, appears to be the second deer!" Apparently, his shot had hit it, but its momentum had carried it down the hill until it fell onto the road.

Glad that he hadn't shot another deer while on his walk with Badger, we quickly dressed the animal, which he then dragged the rest of the way to the truck.

Having harvested six geese and two mule deer, our "mixed bag" hunt had been a great success. We ate a quick lunch, packed up, and headed for home with Badger happily asleep on the floorboard at my feet and Randy still jabbering about "those bouncing deer!"

Venison Goose Liver Pate

As most hunters know, venison is very lean. That leanness sometimes makes it challenging to come up with creative ways to prepare it, but after some trials and errors, I adapted a recipe that uses ground venison and beef or pork, and goose livers to arrive at a delicious, if somewhat complex, appetizer that our guests love!

Pre-Cooking Meat Preparation

Carefully trim the venison and goose livers of all fat and connective tissues, plus any bloodshot tissue. Cut the meats into 1" square cubes, then place the cubes in the freezer on a plate or in a plastic bag to chill until they are fairly firm to the touch, but not completely frozen. When they firm to the touch, remove them from the freezer and grind them with a coarse blade into a large, non-reactive mixing bowl. Add 1 Tbsp each of kosher salt and coarsely ground black pepper and ½ cup cold water as you hand-mix the meat and fat together. Set aside when thoroughly mixed.

Now, cut a piece of cardboard to fit just inside the rim of a 1½ to 2 quart rectangle meatloaf pan and wrap the cardboard with aluminum foil. Set aside.

Ingredients:
- 3 Tbsp olive oil
- 1 medium yellow onion, diced
- 1 shallot, diced
- 3 garlic cloves, minced
- 2 Tbsp tomato paste
- 3/4 cup chicken soup base

Preparation:
1. Heat the oil in a large saute pan over medium heat until shimmering, then add the onion, shallot and garlic and saute until they soften – about 5 minutes. Add the tomato paste and soup base, then bring the liquid to a boil and cook until it reduces to just moist. Remove the pan from the burner and allow the mixture to cool to room temperature.

- 10 oz thick-cut smoked bacon
- 1 lb ground venison and beef or pork mixture
- ½ cup cold water
- ½ lb goose (or chicken) livers, trimmed and diced or pulsed lightly in a food processor'
- 3 tsp kosher salt
- 1 tsp fresh ground pepper
- ¾ tsp ground allspice
- ¾ cup Madeira or brandy
- 3 large eggs, lightly beaten
- 1½ cup bread crumbs
- ~12 strips of thin-sliced bacon
- 2 bay leaves
- 1 large sprig of fresh thyme

2. While the mixture cools, cut the smoked bacon into ½" cubes and par-freeze them (as you did the meat), then pulse it in a food processor until ground but not paste-like. Mix the ground bacon with the meat mixture in a large, nonreactive bowl. Add the livers, salt, pepper, allspice, liquor, and the cooled onion mixture. Then add the eggs and bread crumbs, and mix everything together gently but thoroughly. Your hands work best to avoid over-mixing! Pre-heat the oven to 325°F. While the oven is warming, you can test the flavor by cooking a small patty of the mixture on both sides in a small pan until it is medium-well done. Add more salt or pepper to the uncooked meat mixture if needed.

3. Line a meatloaf pan with the thin-sliced bacon by laying them, overlapping one another, cross-ways across the pan, letting the ends hang over the sides of the pan. If the strips aren't long enough, lengthen them by placing your two index fingers at the center of each strip and gently pressing down on the bacon as you slide your fingers outward. Cut two more bacon strips in half to cover each end of the pan.

4. Fill the pan with the meat mixture, then gently 'tap' the pan on the counter top to help the mixture settle. Place the bay leaves and the thyme spring on top of the mixture, then fold the ends of the bacon strips onto the top of the mixture. Lay the remaining strips of bacon over the top of the entire loaf, then cover the top of the pan with foil.

5. Place the meatloaf pan in the center of a larger pan filled with warm water so that the water comes about halfway up the sides of the meatloaf pan (but make sure it is well below the rim of the larger pan). Place the pans into the oven and bake until the juices of the pate nun clear and the internal temperature registers 140°F – about 90 to 110 minutes. Remove the pans from the oven, remove the meatloaf pan from the larger pan and remove the foil and the top slices of bacon. Cool for at least 30 minutes at room temperature.

6. Place the aluminum-covered cardboard on top of the pate, then weight it down with two or more cans of vegetables or a foil-covered brick. Refrigerate the weighted pate overnight to compress the mixture so that it will hold together.
7. The next day, remove the pate from the refrigerator and run a knife between the pan and the outer layer of bacon. Invert the pan over a cutting board or a platter. If it does not come out easily, return the pan to an upright position, then place it in a shallow hot water bath that comes about ¾ of the way up the sides of the pan for about 30 seconds, then invert again over the cutting board and it should slide out. Gently scrape the sides of the pate with the back of a dinner knife [or use your hands] to remove all excess fat.
8. With a thin, sharp knife, cut the pate into ¼" slices. Wrap each slice [except those you plan to serve immediately!] in foil and freeze for up to six months. Serve as an appetizer with capers and stone ground or Dijon mustard on small toasts.

Sliced Beefsteak Tomatoes and Walla Walla Onions with Creamy Bleu Cheese Dressing

Ingredients:

- 2 large beefsteak tomatoes, washed and chilled, then cut crosswise into ¼-inch slices
- 1 large Walla Walla (or Vidalia) onion, washed and chilled, then cut crosswise into ¼-inch slices
- ¾ cup creamy Bleu cheese dress (recipe below)
- 1 tbsp. chopped fresh chives

Preparation:

1. Arrange sliced tomatoes and sliced onions on a serving platter in two parallel rows, overlapping halfway.
2. Drizzle dressing (recipe below) over tomatoes and onions, sprinkle with chives, and serve.

Venison Osso Buco

Ingredients:

- 1 sprig fresh rosemary
- 1 sprig fresh thyme
- 2 bay leaves
- 6 whole cloves
- Cheesecloth
- Kitchen twine, for bouquet garni and tying the veal shanks
- 4 whole venison shanks (about 1 pound per shank), trimmed of fat and visible gristle
- Sea salt and freshly ground black pepper, to taste
- ½ cup all purpose flour, for dredging
- ½ cup vegetable oil
- 1 medium yellow onion, coarsely chopped
- 1 small carrot, coarsely chopped
- 2 stalks celery, coarsely chopped
- 1 Tbsp tomato paste
- 1 cup dry white wine
- One can (28 oz) of diced tomatoes
- 3 cups chicken soup base or stock
- 3 Tbsps fresh flat-leaf Italian parsley, chopped
- 1 tablespoon lemon zest

Preparation:

1. Place the rosemary, thyme, bay leaf and cloves into cheesecloth and secure with twine.
2. Pat the venison shanks dry with paper towels to remove any excess moisture. Secure the meat to the bone with the kitchen twine. Season each shank with salt and freshly ground pepper, then dredge the shanks in flour, shaking off any excess flour.
3. In a large heavy-bottomed soup pot, heat the vegetable oil until shimmering. Place the shanks into the pot and brown all over – about 3 minutes per side. Remove the browned shanks and set aside.
4. Place the onion, carrot and celery into the same pot and season with salt (to help draw the moisture out of the vegetables). Sautee until soft and translucent – about 8 minutes. Add the tomato paste and mix well. Return the shanks to the pan, then add the wine. Bring the liquid to a low boil, then simmer until it reduces by half – about 5 minutes. Add the bouquet garni, the tomatoes and 2 cups of the chicken stock. Bring the mixture to a boil, then reduce the heat to low, cover pan and simmer for about one and a half hours. Check frequently, turning the shanks and adding more stock as needed to keep the amount of liquid more than half way up the shank. Remove from the heat when the meat easily falls from the bone.
5. Carefully remove the shanks from the pot and place them in a wide, shallow serving bowl. Cut off and discard the twine.
6. Remove the bouquet garni from the pot.
7. Pour all of the remaining juices and sauce over the shanks. Garnish with the chopped parsley and lemon zest

Mushroom Risotto

Ingredients:

- 2 qt. chicken soup base or stock
- 1 tbsp. extra virgin olive oil
- 4 slices of bacon, chopped into ¼-inch pieces
- 2 cups medium-grain rice
- 1 cup shiitake or baby portabella mushrooms, stems removed, cut crosswise into ¼-inch slices
- 1 cup fat-free sour cream
- 1 cup grated parmesan cheese

Preparation:

1. Heat the chicken soup base or stock to a simmer, then keep it at a constant simmer.
2. In a large, heavy-bottomed stockpot, heat the oil over medium heat. Add the bacon and cook for 4 minutes until lightly browned. Add the onion and cook, stirring constantly for 6 minutes. Add the minced garlic and cook for 2 minutes or until fragrant.
3. Add the rice and stir until it is coated with fat, then add the wine and cook, stirring constantly, until the pan is nearly dry—about 3 minutes.
4. Add 1 cup of the stock to the rice and cook, stirring, until the stock is absorbed—about 2 minutes.
5. Gradually add more stock, ¾ cup at a time, and stir gently until absorbed before adding more.
6. After 15 to 18 minutes, taste the rice for firmness and flavor, and add less stock at a time until the rice reaches the preferred texture.
7. Add the sliced mushrooms to the rice and mix thoroughly. Then add the sour cream and 1 cup of the parmesan cheese. Taste, and add salt and pepper if needed.
8. Stir gently for 5 or 6 minutes, and sprinkle in the chives.
9. Spoon the risotto into a large bowl and serve with the remaining parmesan cheese.

Creamy Bleu Cheese Dressing

Ingredients:

- ¼ cup Stilton Bleu cheese
- 2 tbsp. 2% milk (or buttermilk)
- 3 tbsp. fat free sour cream
- 2 tbsp. reduced fat mayonnaise
- 1 tbsp. white wine vinegar
- ¼ tsp. sugar
- ½ tsp. granulated garlic
- kosher salt and freshly ground black pepper, to taste

Preparation:

1. In a small bowl, mash the Bleu cheese and milk together with a fork until the mixture has the consistency of large-curd cottage cheese. Stir in the sour cream, mayonnaise, vinegar, sugar, and granulated garlic until well blended. Season to taste with the salt and pepper.

Suggested Accompaniment

- *Zinfandel:* James Creek Vineyard—St. Helena, California, or Dancing Bull—Modesto, California

Venison Osso Buco

I Got My Goat or
(It Got Me)

For my birthday early in September 1987, I received the best present I could imagine—a lottery-draw tag for a Rocky Mountain goat. Only four tags were available in the area that year due to increasing predation on the goats by mountain lions. Even though they hadn't drawn tags, my good friends Don and Ken had each taken goats out of the same rocky crags in years past, so they knew the area and the goats' habits, and were almost as excited as I was to embark on this quest.

I spent September with a weighted pack hiking trails near my suburban Seattle-area home, and when October arrived, I was ready for the challenge of the hunt. The hunting area was thirteen miles from the trailhead at an elevation of six thousand feet, and was filled with talus chutes and outcroppings that we'd have to climb to get to the goats—probably in lousy weather.

Don and I headed out with the sun on our backs, and the air crisp and clean. We hiked the first seven miles to a natural hot spring where we pitched camp and began gathering firewood. Don and I had different ideas about how to get the wood back to our campsite, and as I stepped out from behind a tree with an armload of branches, I felt a "smack" between my eyes and dropped to the ground. Don had decided to throw, rather than carry, his branches back to the fire pit!

Don irrigated and bandaged the wound, then urged me to join him in the hot spring. It soothed our hike-sore muscles, but the 35-degree night air sure made us catch our breaths when we stepped, naked, out of the warm water!

The next morning, over my protests, Don insisted that we hike back down to the car and drive to a nearby town to have it stitched up. After several "poor widdle city boy" jibes from the doctor—who was used to sewing up loggers' chainsaw and ax injuries—we headed back up the trail and picked up where we left off, continuing another six miles into steeper and less-traveled terrain. We emerged in lush alpine meadows with crystal-clear streams surrounded by soaring rock cliffs and made camp for the night—with no firewood this time. The next morning greeted us with blue skies and a dusting of snow that was beautiful but not ideal for spotting snow-white goats! Fortunately, the snow dissipated by mid-morning, and we glassed the area from several vantage points, including a ridge that looked onto the bottom of a glacier and into a couple of very promising canyons. The goats just weren't there, as it was probably still too warm for them at this elevation.

Because of Don's work schedule, he wasn't able to go with me again. The last weekend of the season, though, Don's brother Ken was available and eager. When I picked him up late on that Friday afternoon, he sounded terrible and confessed that he was "not quite over" a bout of bronchitis. Nevertheless, hacking all the way, he set an incredibly fast pace up the trail to the hot springs—by flashlight! We pitched our tent on the side of a babbling brook and watched a meteor shower as we fell asleep.

Up the trail before light the next morning, we pitched our base camp in the same place as before, then headed immediately across the meadow to a rock wall leading up to where Ken had killed a goat three years earlier. As we strapped on our climbing crampons, Ken looked across to the far end of the wall and said, almost as if he was just thinking out loud, "There are two goats. Let's take a closer look at them." We extracted our binoculars and tripods—his a 15×60— and studied the animals. After a few minutes, Ken said, "The one on the right is a nanny with about nine-inch horns, and the one on the left is a billy with about seven-and-a-half-inch horns. The nanny is leaving, but the billy is going to bed down. Let's go get *your* goat." I'll never forget those words—he had no doubt that we would cross the rock wall and kill that goat!

Stopping several times along the way to make sure that the bedded goat hadn't moved, it took us about two hours to get to within stalking range. Moving quietly across the rocks, we crept up to a large boulder. "He should be about fifty yards on the other side of this rock," Ken whispered. Creeping forward and peeking over the rock, Ken said, "Use my shoulder as your rest. He's *right there!*" And there he was, less than twenty-five yards away, stretching as he rose from his nap. My .300 Win Mag barked, and the goat fell to its knees, but quickly recovered and ran toward the edge of the rock wall. Another shot put him down for good, but as he slumped to the ground, he rolled over in slow motion—off the side of the wall!

Although the goat had tumbled nearly a hundred yards down the wall to its base, it had not suffered from the ordeal. We noted that it was almost three o'clock and that darkness would soon be upon us, so we shot a few quick photos, then skinned and deboned my trophy. Navigating the loose rocks and thick brush as we headed toward the stream above our camp was not easy. Loose rocks and slippery moss made the going treacherous. I nearly lost Ken (and my arm sockets as I held on to his belt with my left hand and wrapped my right arm around a tree) as he forged the stream. We eventually made it in one piece, more or less, and thoroughly enjoyed some freeze-dried stew cooked on a propane stove before falling into an exhausted slumber.

The next morning, we packed up and tore down the mountain with nearly a hundred pounds each, covering all thirteen miles in just over four and a half hours!

Now that I had my trophy goat, I realized that I knew nothing about cooking it. Would it be like venison? Its forage was nothing like a deer's forage—mostly lichen, with some grasses and mosses—and the terrain in which it lived would surely cause it to be muscular and stringy, right?

Right, unfortunately! It was very lean (and tough), and a little on the gamy side. Further, in 1987, there was no Internet, and calls to a number of libraries, bookstores, and friends (including Don and Ken) yielded next to nothing in the way of suggestions. Fortunately, after many trials and more than a few serious errors, I arrived at a recipe that relies on marinating and gentle cooking.

Sweet Onion Bisque

Ingredients:

- 6 cups sweet onions, peeled and sliced
- 5 tbsp. butter or margarine
- 1–2 cups fat free Half-and-Half
- kosher salt and medium, ground white pepper, to taste
- 2 slices smoked bacon, cooked until crispy, then drained and crumbled
- chopped chives (to garnish)

Preparation:

1. Simmer onions in butter over very low heat in a 4-quart stockpot for at least 2½ hours.
2. Transfer to a blender and puree until smooth. Add Half-and-Half to taste.
3. Return to the pot to reheat. Season with salt and white pepper to taste, then ladle into individual soup bowls, garnish with bacon and chives and serve.

Roasted Root Vegetable Salad with Toasted Walnuts

Ingredients:

- 2 each medium red, gold, or yellow beets, and turnips, washed and drained, with stems trimmed
- 4 tbsp. olive oil, divided
- ¼ cup balsamic vinegar
- kosher salt and coarsely ground black pepper, to taste
- 2 cups curly endive leaves, washed and drained then torn into bite-sized pieces
- 1 cup watercress leaves, washed and drained
- 3 tbsp. grated orange peel
- ½ cup toasted walnuts, coarsely chopped

Preparation:

1. Preheat the oven to 350°F.
2. Rub each vegetable with some oil and place them on a cookie sheet, then bake them until they are tender when pierced with a fork—about 45 minutes.
3. Remove the vegetables from the oven and let rest until cool enough to handle, then peel and cut them into ¼ discs. Transfer the pieces to a bowl or dish, then cover and set aside.
4. Place the walnuts in a small casserole dish and bake for 10 minutes. Transfer to a cutting board and chop coarsely.
5. Whisk the vinegar, salt, and pepper together in a small mixing bowl, then slowly add 2 tablespoons of the oil while whisking until fully blended.
6. Mix the endive and watercress leaves together, then transfer to individual salad plates, top with the vegetable discs, and garnish with the chopped walnuts and the orange zest. Serve immediately.

Marinated Mountain Goat Backstrap
with Roasted Vegetable Confit

Marinade Ingredients:

- ½ tsp. chili powder
- ½ tsp. cumin
- ½ tsp. coriander
- ½ tsp. fennel seeds
- 2 tbsp. dried oregano
- 1 tbsp. granulated garlic
- ¼ cup extra-virgin olive oil
- ½ cup red wine vinegar
- ½ tbsp. brown sugar
- 1 tsp. sweet paprika
- Salt and black pepper to taste
- mountain goat backstrap

Confit Ingredients:

- 1 pt. cherry tomatoes
- ½ lb. pearl onions
- ½ lb. mushrooms, quartered
- 4 whole garlic cloves
- 1 cup fresh tarragon, chopped
- ½ cup fresh oregano, chopped
- ½ cup olive oil
- 1 tsp. sea salt

Preparation:

1. Slice the backstraps lengthwise into strips about ½-inch thick. Roll them up and tie with cooking twine.
2. Mix the marinade ingredients in a bowl; spoon over the meat rolls in a glass casserole dish, then cover and marinate overnight in the fridge.
3. Remove the meat from the marinade. Keep the marinade to use to finish the oven cooking.
4. In a frying pan, sear the rolls of meat in olive oil and set aside.
5. To make the confit, pre-heat the oven to 250°C and put the pearl onions, mushrooms, and garlic cloves, coated with 1–2 tablespoons of the olive oil, in a single layer on a baking tray and cook for 20 minutes.
6. Add the tomatoes and cook another 15 minutes. Add the rest of the olive oil, the oregano, basil, sea salt, and pepper. Bake another 20 minutes.
7. Increase the oven temperature to 300°C to finish cooking the meat rolls. Use a cooking brush to add more of the marinade mix and cook for another 20 minutes or until the meat is pale pink inside.
8. Leave for five minutes before cutting. Serve the meat rolls on a bed of confit.

Suggested Accompaniment

- *Malbec:* Alamos—Catena Valley, Argentina, or Montes—Colchagua Valley, Chile

Marinated Mountain Goat* Backstrap with Roasted Vegetable Confit
* Domestic Goat substituted

Tide Pool Treasures

Children walking hand-in-hand with mom and dad, racing about on their stubby little legs, are what a trip to the seashore is all about. The warm summer sun, twinkling and sparkling off the surf rhythmically rolling down long stretches of smooth sand, makes the world wonderful and magical.

It was with these thoughts in mind that my wife, Susan, and I accepted an offer from her brother to rent a beach house at Cannon Beach, Oregon, for a long weekend in late June 1988. Although the weather along the Pacific coast can be problematic until later in the summer, we were eager to get away from the grind and introduce our five-year-old son, Luke, and three-year-old daughter, Meagan, to the ocean.

We left our home in south Seattle early on a Friday morning under clear, blue skies (remember Perry Como's '70s 'hit' song "The Bluest Skies You've Ever Seen Are in Seattle"?). And after patiently plowing through some rush hour congestion as we approached Tacoma, Seattle's smaller cousin at the south end of Puget Sound, we made good time to Portland, then west to the coast along the Columbia River. That section of Oregon features hills and ridges rising steeply from the water's edge to an elevation of a thousand to fifteen hundred feet or more, making the drive both breathtaking and a bit scary at times.

After arriving at the small but cozy beachside house, we unpacked and saw that the tide was high, leaving very little beach to enjoy, so we ate lunch at a nearby diner and let the kids each pick out a souvenir before heading back to the beach.

We changed into beach combing togs—T-shirts, shorts, and old, low-cut tennis shoes—then raced the kids from the cottage to the water's edge. Although the tide was still receding, it was amazing to see how much beach had been exposed since we had arrived, and Meagan squealed with delight when she found a sand dollar.

"Daddy! Isn't it pretty?" she said in her little voice. "Can I keep it?"

"Yes, you can!" I answered, holding out a small pail so she could put her treasure in it. As she was putting the shell gently into the pail, Luke shouted, "I found a gigantic clam, Mom!"

Meggie raced off to see what he had found, and Susan and I smiled watching the kids have fun. When we reached Luke and his "gigantic clam," we quickly saw that he wasn't kidding. He had found a dead but still intact geoduck (pronounced "goo-ee duck")—a large member of the clam family that can weigh up to ten pounds! Luke's trophy clam was eight or nine inches long and nearly six inches in diameter!

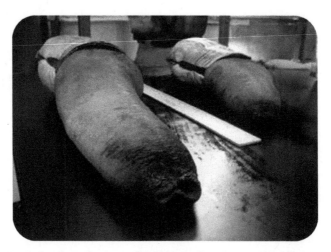

Geoduck – Photo Courtesy of Washington Department of Fish & Game

"Can we keep it, Dad?" he asked eagerly.

"Yes. But I'll have to take out the clam or it will stink!" I responded as he dropped it into the bucket.

Further on were some large rocks that had been exposed as the tide receded. I was pretty sure that we would be able to find some hermit crabs and starfish in the tide pools on top of the rocks. Dozens of small crabs scurried away as we approached, hiding under loose rocks and overhanging rock ledges; and we found barnacles, limpets, snails, and various tiny fish. As the tide continued to expose more rocks, we carefully ventured farther out and soon found even deeper tide pools. Susan didn't want Meggie that far out on the rocks where a slip or a rogue wave could wash her out to sea, so she and Meggie continued to play in the shallower pools while Luke and I explored the deeper pools.

In one fairly deep pool, several starfish clung to the rocks. Two were slate gray, one was brown, and the other was orange.

"How come they're different colors?" Luke asked.

"I'm not sure," I responded. "That's just how they are!"

I also noticed that of several of the larger rocks were covered with huge clusters of mussels, some nearly three inches long! Susan and I love mussels, so I decided that I'd come back and get some before we left.

Before long, the kids began to tire, so we called it an afternoon and crossed the beach toward our cabin.

We awoke the next morning to low tide and decided to find some clams for dinner that night. As we looked over the smooth, empty beach, Luke asked, "How do we find the clams?"

"Look for tiny holes in the sand. When they dig down into the sand, they leave an air hole." I answered.

"Here's one!" he shouted. I ran to him with our small shovel in hand and started digging next to the hole. A short time later, with a small mound of sand heaped beside me, Luke reached down into the hole and grabbed two two-inch-long butter clams.

"Great job!" I told him as he laid them in our bucket.

"I want to catch one!" Meggie squealed as she saw the clams and decided that they wouldn't hurt her.

"See if you can find a hole in the sand like Luke did," Susan responded.

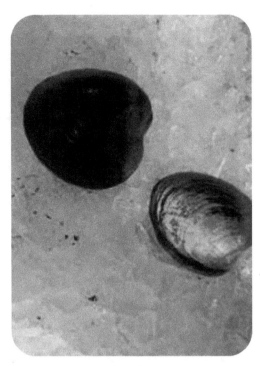
Butter Clams

She did, and we eventually found a dozen clams and a geoduck before the tide chased us back up the beach.

The sun glistened on the waves. We soon found our way back to the rocky tide pools, and the kids were just as happy and fascinated at what they saw as if this was the first time they'd seen a tide pool. Crabs, colorful snails, sea urchins, and darting blennies kept them occupied for nearly an hour as the kids explored one pools after another.

As the kids began to grow bored with their explorations, I decided that it would be a good time to harvest a handful of mussels before we headed back to the cabin. I had found a short piece of metal and kept it to help pry loose a few of the mollusks from the rocks.

The best place to pry some loose was below the water line as far out on the rocks as possible, so I carefully lowered myself into waist deep water. Then, using the metal bar, I selected a bunch of healthy, purplish mussels clinging firmly to the rocks about a foot below the water's surface. Working the lever in a small circle, I was able to pry a cluster from the rock and drop them into the pail.

Mussels – Photo Courtesy of Washington Department of Fish & Game

When I hoisted myself back up onto the rocks, I showed Susan and the kids my harvest—about three dozen large, beautiful mussels! We had all found a tide pool treasure that weekend on a gorgeous beach on the coast of Oregon.

Cannon Beach – Photo Courtesy of Oregon Department of Parks & Recreation

Shellfish Chowder

Ingredients:

- 2 qt. water
- ½ stick butter
- 1 pound Yukon Gold potatoes, peeled and cut into ½-inch cubes
- ½ cup celery, diced
- ½ cup onion, diced
- ¼ cup carrot, diced
- ¾ cup all-purpose flour
- 2 cups clam broth
- 6 cups yogurt (low fat or non-fat is okay)
- 1 tsp. dried thyme
- ½ tsp. dried dill
- 1 tbsp. kosher salt
- 1 tsp. ground white pepper
- 2 bay leaves (optional)
- 1 lb. clams, mussels and geoducks*, chopped, with juices
- 2 tbsp. fresh flat-leafed parsley or chives (or a combination), chopped

* Optional.

Preparation:

1. Boil 2 quarts water in a medium stockpot, then boil the geoducks for 10 minutes. Remove, cool enough to handle, and remove the mantle (body) from the shell, then separate the siphon from the mantle, peel the skin from the siphon, and chop coarsely.
2. In a 6-quart stockpot over medium-high heat, melt the butter, then add the potatoes, celery, onion, and carrot; and sauté until tender—5 or 6 minutes.
3. Add the flour and stir until a roux forms.
4. Add the clam broth, yogurt, thyme, dill, salt, pepper, and bay leaves, then bring the mixture to a boil, stirring constantly.
5. Reduce the heat to a simmer and cook until the potatoes are tender—about 20 minutes.
6. Add the clams/mussels/geoduck and stir until fully integrated. Continue to simmer for another 15 to 20 minutes, then transfer to a serving bowl and sprinkle on the parsley or chives (or both).

Sparkling Tangelos

Ingredients:

- ½ cup sugar
- ½ cup orange marmalade
- 1 cup champagne
- 8 tangelos, peeled and sectioned
- ½ cup toasted slivered almonds

Preparation:

1. In a small saucepan over medium heat, combine the sugar and marmalade; and cook, stirring, until the sugar dissolves. Remove from the heat and let cool for 10 minutes.
2. Place the tangelo piece, the sugar mixture, and the champagne in a medium mixing bowl and toss gently, then cover and chill for 6 to 8 hours.
3. Fill individual compote dishes with the mixture and sprinkle with the toasted almonds. Serve immediately.

Crusty Artisan Bread

Ingredients:

- 1½ tbsp. dry yeast
- 1½ tbsp. coarse grey sea salt
- 3 cups warm water
- 6½ cups unbleached, all-purpose flour, plus more for dusting
- 1 tbsp. cornmeal

Preparation:

1. In a large bowl, mix the yeast and salt into the 3 cups of warm water. Once the water begins to foam, add the flour and stir to combine completely.
2. Let the dough rise, covered in a warm place for at least 2 hours, until it rises and collapses—up to 5 hours. The dough may be baked at this point, or refrigerated for later use.
3. Cover the dough, but make sure it is not airtight so that gases can escape—and place it in the refrigerator until you are ready to use it.
4. Dust a flat, clean surface with flour and use a serrated knife to cut off a grapefruit-sized piece of dough. Turning the dough in your hands, stretch the surface of the dough and tuck in under so that the surface is smooth and the bottom is bunched.
5. Sprinkle the flat surface with cornmeal and roll the dough in it. Allow the dough to rest in a warm place for 40 minutes— longer if you make a larger loaf.
6. Twenty minutes before baking, preheat the oven to 450°F with a baking stone or overturned baking sheet inside on the middle rack and a shallow metal pan on the top rack. Dust the top of the dough with a small fistful of flour, slash it in a cross, a tic-tac-toe, or a fan), and place it on the baking stone. Pour 1–2 cups of tap water into the metal pan on the top rack and quickly shut the oven door to trap steam inside. Bake for 30 minutes, or until the crust is well browned and the bread sounds hollow when you rap it on the bottom with your knuckles.

Sweet GingerCarrot Salad

Ingredients:

- 1 lb. carrots, shredded
- 2 tbsp. apple cider vinegar
- 1 tbsp. vegetable oil
- 2 tbsp. honey
- 1 clove garlic, grated
- ¼ tsp. ground cumin
- ¼ tsp. ground cinnamon
- 1 tsp. grated fresh ginger
- ½ tsp. grey sea salt
- ⅛ tsp. cayenne pepper
- ½ cup chopped dates

Preparation:

1. Whisk the vinegar, oil, honey, and garlic together in a large mixing bowl.
2. Add the cumin, cinnamon, ginger, salt, and cayenne and mix thoroughly.
3. Combine the carrots and dates in a large bowl and toss with the dressing.
4. Cover, and refrigerate at least 4 hours before serving.

Suggested Accompaniment

- *Sauvignon Blanc:* Marlborough Estate "Zeal"— New Zealand

Shellfish Chowder & Artisan Bread

Western Walleyes

It was a happy coincidence that my wife and I had scheduled our spring vacation at Lake Chelan, Washington, the same week as our friends Don and Cindy had scheduled theirs at nearby Banks Lake. Don, an avid bass fisherman, wanted me to fish with him; and our wives, long-time friends from college, agreed we would all have fun.

The forecast for that week April 1988, called for temperatures in the seventies. Our drive from Seattle to Lake Chelan through the Cascades was beautiful as we climbed out of the clouds of western Washington then dropped down the eastern slopes into bright sunshine. The kids were anxious to get to the lake, but they insisted that we stop at Rocky Reach Dam on the Columbia River north of Wenatchee to see the wild guinea pigs. Apparently, some knuckleheads had decided to dump their unwanted pets at the park, and the critters had not only survived but had multiplied to over a hundred! Dozens of low-lying juniper bushes provided shade from the summer heat and shelter from predators (including curious children), and the rodents were thriving.

One of the unique bounties we had discovered on past visits to the area was wild asparagus. If the weather cooperated with mild temperatures and enough rain to kickstart growth, we could pick as much as we could eat along roadsides and a couple of open fields just outside the city limits of Chelan. This year was especially good, and we picked as much as we could eat while saving some for our visit with our friends later in the week. After an hour's drive, we arrived at the Coulee Dam Playland Resort around ten o'clock Wednesday morning. Just south of the town of Grand Coulee and the Grand Coulee Dam, the resort sat on the northeastern shore of Banks Lake. Don, a member of the Bass Angler's Sportsmen's Society (BASS), was entered in the American Bass Angler's Tournament Trail event that year.

We pulled into the parking lot of the resort where dozens of bass boats—some of which were clearly very expensive, with large outboard engines, metallic paint jobs, and a multitude of fishing lure and rod manufacturers' decals plastered on the sides were parked. As Don explained later, sponsorships were a by-product of the tournament circuit for successful anglers. The grand prize for this tournament, for example, was $10,000 and a fully equipped bass boat! The tournament didn't start until Friday, so we would just be locating spots for Don to fish later. We would start on the shallower east shoreline, work our way around Steamboat Rock, then move to several areas on the west shoreline as the afternoon sun slid below the edge of the steep basalt cliffs that protected the deep, colder water of that side of the lake.

With our families happily situated in the resort's playground area, Don and I set out in his flat-bottomed boat. It was an older boat that he had reconditioned himself, but it was outfitted with a full array of electronic gadgets that put him on par with his more affluent competitors.

As I mentioned, I am not a bass fisherman; so as we approached a small cove almost a mile from the dock, I had a bunch of questions for Don: what kind of lures will we be using? Will the fish be in deep or shallow water? Will there be anything other than bass?

He patiently answered my questions by explaining that the bass were just starting to "bed up" and were very protective of their nesting beds, so our approach would be to present threats to the females—salamanders, leeches, predator fish, etc.—in an effort to get them to attack the intruder.

As Don cut the engine and we coasted into the shallow water of the cove, we could see the shadows of fish of various sizes skitter toward cover, and Don was psyched. He caught several fish in short order while I caught various plants, sticks, and underwater obstacles.

"Time to move to our next spot!" Don said, not concerned that I was still fishless. We reeled up and headed for the east side of Steamboat Rock—a rock formation on a narrow peninsula about a third of the way down and jutting out about three hundred yards from the eastern shoreline of the lake. Don explained that here, the bass would be cruising under overhanging trees looking for frogs, small snakes, and lizards that had fallen into the lake; so we would be fishing with top-water lures and spinner baits.

Steamboat Rock – Photo Courtesy of Washington Parks Department

All went according to Don's plans as we cast to within a few inches of the rocky shore, and I was eventually rewarded for my efforts when I hooked a feisty four-pound, small-mouth bass! An hour later, Don suggested that we re-rig our rods for walleye before heading to the west side of the lake.

"Walleye?" I asked, not realizing that Banks Lake held any of the species.

"Yep. Banks Lake has a pretty good population, and they're fun to catch—and eat—if you know how to fish for them!" Don replied. "They hang out fairly deep, so we'll have to troll slowly with about two ounces of weight."

He quickly attached two gold spinners trailing bright yellow and bright lime-green plastic "worms" on size 2–ought Mustad hooks, and both lures were quickly trailing behind as we headed across the lake. A hundred yards later, the rod with the lure at a depth of seventy feet jerked in its rod holder. I quickly grabbed the rod to set the hook, but the fish was gone.

I let out more line, figuring that the fish might be deeper than we thought. We continued our slow troll toward the far shoreline, and moments later, my rod jerked spasmodically. I grabbed it and, feeling the resistance of the fish on the other end of the line, lowered the rod tip a little before yanking it skyward to set the hook.

Don quickly shifted the outboard to idle and began to reel in his lure. Almost instantly, another fish grabbed it and headed straight away from the boat.

Having never played a walleye, I decided to be a little cautious, so Don got his fish into the boat before I boated mine.

Walleye – Image Courtesy of Wisconsin Department of Wildlife

The bass fishing on the west side turned out to be unproductive, but Don had learned what he would need to know when the tournament started, and we had two beautiful western walleyes and lots of fresh asparagus for dinner.

Warm BaconWrapped Asparagus on Toast with Balsamic Vinaigrette

Ingredients:

- 1 tbsp. aged balsamic vinegar
- ½ tsp. Dijon mustard
- 3 tbsp. extra-virgin olive oil
- 3 tbsp. butter, melted, divided
- grey sea salt and coarsely ground black pepper, to taste
- ½ lb. (about 8 to 10 slices) thin-sliced smoked bacon
- 1 lb. fresh asparagus spears, washed and drained, with tough ends trimmed
- four ½ inch-thick slices Italian bread, toasted

Preparation:

1. Preheat the oven to 450°F.
2. Whisk the balsamic and mustard together in small bowl, then gradually whisk in the oil and 1 tablespoon of the melted butter.
3. Season with salt and pepper to taste.
4. Place a paper towel on a plate, then place the bacon strips on the paper towel. Microwave the bacon for a minute and a half until partially cooked, but still soft enough to wrap around the bacon. Let cool for handling.
5. Roll three or four asparagus spears in each bacon slice and place on a rimmed baking sheet. Bake until the bacon is crisp—about 18 to 20 minutes.
6. Toast the bread slices, then brush with the remaining melted butter.
7. Arrange two toasts on each of 4 plates, then lay an asparagus spears on top of each toast and drizzle with vinaigrette and serve immediately.

PanFried Walleye Fillets in Honeyed Batter

Ingredients:

- 2 large eggs
- 3 tbsp. honey, divided
- 1 cup crushed "club" crackers
- 1/3 cup flour
- kosher salt and coarsely ground black pepper, to taste
- Four 6 oz. walleye fillets (about 1–1/2 lb.)
- sunflower oil

Preparation:

1. In a shallow mixing bowl, beat the eggs and 2 tbsp of the honey together until thoroughly blended.
2. In a separate mixing bowl, combine the cracker crumbs and flour, plus salt and pepper to taste.
3. Dip each fillet into the egg-honey mixture, then dredge in the crumb mixture.
4. In a large sauté pan, heat ¼-inch of oil over medium-high heat until shimmering, then add the fillets and cook for 3 to 4 minutes on each side or until fish flakes easily with a fork.
5. Transfer the fillets to a serving platter and drizzle with the additional honey

Chilled Red Potato Salad

Ingredients:

- 3 lb. small red potatoes
- kosher salt, to taste
- 1 cup reduced-fat mayonnaise
- ¼ cup non-fat Half-and-Half
- 2 tbsp. Dijon mustard
- 2 tbsp. stone-ground mustard
- ½ cup chopped fresh fennel fronds
- freshly ground black pepper, to taste
- 3 hardboiled eggs, cut crosswise into ⅛-inch slices
- ½ cup celery, coarsely chopped
- ½ cup scallion, coarsely chopped

Preparation:

1. Place the potatoes and some salt in a 4-quart stockpot of water. Bring the water to a boil, then lower the heat and cook for 10 to 15 minutes—until the potatoes are just tender when pierced with a fork.
2. Pour the potatoes into a colander to drain, then place the colander over the empty pot and cover it with a dry kitchen towel for 20 minutes.
3. While the potatoes are steaming, stir the mayonnaise, Half-and-Half, mustards, and fennel together, and add salt and pepper to taste. Set aside.
4. When the potatoes are cool enough to handle, cut them into ½-inch cubes and place them in a large mixing bowl. While the potatoes are still warm, pour the dressing over them and stir gently to moisten all of the cubes. If needed, add more dressing as the salad sits.
5. When the potatoes and dressing have rested for about 20 minutes, gently stir in the celery and scallions, plus a little more salt and pepper, to taste.
6. Toss all of the ingredients except the egg slices thoroughly, then cover and refrigerate the salad for a few hours (to allow the flavors to come together).
7. Remove the salad from the refrigerator, top with the egg slices, and serve chilled.

Sauted Yellow Squash and Sweet Onions

Ingredients:

- 3 tbsp. extra-virgin olive oil
- 1 tbsp. butter
- ¼ tsp. cayenne pepper
- 4 cups yellow squash, washed, drained, and cut crosswise into thin slices
- 4 cups sweet onions, peeled, halved, and cut crosswise into thin slices
- kosher salt and coarsely ground black pepper, to taste.

Preparation:

1. Heat the oil and butter in a large sauté pan over medium heat until shimmering.
2. Add the cayenne pepper, stirring, then add the squash and onion slices. Cook, stirring occasionally, until tender— about 10 to 12 minutes. Add salt and pepper to taste.
3. Transfer to a serving bowl and serve immediately.

Suggested Accompaniment

- *Chardonnay:* Cambria
- *Sauvignon Blanc:* Jones of Washington – Columbia Valley, Washington

Pan-Fried Walleye in Honeyed Batter with Bacon-wrapped Asparagas

A Family Tradition

Two weeks before my son Luke's ninth birthday in August 1990, my dad invited Luke and me to go fishing at Neah Bay, Washington. The King (or Chinook) salmon had likely already migrated past Neah Bay and headed up the Strait of Juan de Fuca into Puget Sound, but the early stages of the coho (silver) salmon run had started.

Neah Bay is the main hub of the Makah Indian Reservation. It's a small town tucked at the water's edge behind several hilly knolls to the west, so the town escapes much of the wind and surf action off the Strait during Washington's rainy winter. Fortunately, it was usually pleasant from July through early September—the prime months for the migrations of three salmon species—the King, the coho, and the pink or "humpy."

We opted to drive from our homes in south Seattle rather than take a ferry. Including a stop for lunch and gas, it took nearly five hours, but the scenic coastal vistas and lush forests helped us enjoy every mile, and we rolled into Neah Bay in time to see the sun set over the Pacific.

Just before dawn the next morning, we packed lunches, gulped down a quick breakfast, and joined a small crowd of fishermen heading for the docks and their boats. The sights, sounds, and smells have been with me since I was young: big, bright halogen lights that cast shadows into the dark water under the docks and illuminated all manner of boats with diesel and gas engines sputtering and fuming as fishermen laughed and chattered about "the big one" they would catch later that day. Charter boat captains and live-bait vendors added to the singsong rhythm of the morning as we readied for our day on the water.

Several people said that the King run seemed to have petered out. "Oh, well," I said to Dad, "we've caught fish when others couldn't, haven't we?" He couldn't disagree, especially with Luke waiting for his response.

Dawn had broken as we rounded Waddah Island—a small island and jetty that protects Neah Bay from weather and waves—and we knew that the deep, rocky stretch to open waters could hold plenty of fish. As I baited our lines with fresh, plug-cut herring, I noticed a fair-sized bait ball churning the water between us and the rocks. "See if you can run us through that bait school!" I shouted over the growl of the motor. Dad steered the boat directly into the school, and on the third pass, the tip of my rod began a spasmodic dance and line began to peel from the reel.

We had to be very careful not to get too close to the large, jagged rocks—both to avoid hitting them and to prevent the fish from abrading the line. We weren't sure that it was, in fact, a salmon on the line: rockfish, sea bass, ling cod, and other species also inhabit the area. A minute or two later, however, the fish swam away from the rocks and rolled on the surface, revealing that it was, in fact, a salmon! I would have preferred to play the fish lightly and slowly, but Luke convinced me to get it into the boat quickly so that he and Grandpa could catch some too!

The fish was a chunky little six-pound King—little because he barely exceeded the twenty-eight-inch-size minimum—but our day was off to a great start. We trolled the rocky area for another forty-five minutes, then decided to move to another spot. By then, most of the other boats had headed toward Tatoosh Island—on which is located the most northwestern lighthouse in the United States—and beyond. We had no intention of going around the island to an area named Skagway even though the "dock talk" said it was the most likely haunt for any remaining Kings. Instead, we decided to surface troll toward Tatoosh looking for coho, and then come back toward Neah Bay slow-trolling and "mooching" along the rocky shoreline and outcroppings for Kings and bottom fish.

The warming morning sun and the gentle rolling swells coming in from the Pacific soon had us thinking about lunch and a nap. We had managed to pick up three scrappy cohos of about four pounds each, but we wanted to see more salmon action. It was only mid-morning, and we weren't going to let Luke's first foray into ocean fishing end without trying every idea we could think of.

As Dad handed Luke and me each a sandwich and a soda, I reeled in everyone's lines to change our sinkers and put on fresh bait. Dad angled the boat toward a long-ago favorite spot of mine—I'll explain why later—to begin a slow troll and mooching run. I stripped out seventy feet of line from Luke's reel, set the drag, and placed the rod into a rod holder as I began to do the same with my setup. Dad, an old hand at all kinds of fishing, had decided to finish his lunch and answer Luke's many questions, like: "How many fish did my dad catch when he was my age?" and "How big were they?" In the middle of one of his answers, Dad noticed that the tip of Luke's rod had begun to bow—hard! Line began to peel slowly from the reel as I slid the pole out of the pole holder and handed it to Luke, but there wasn't the usual telltale jerking of a hooked fish, so we began to worry that he had snagged bottom. We were nearly a hundred yards from shore, and we knew that the water in this area was at least 120 feet deep, so something just wasn't right.

The only thing that wasn't right was that there was a fish on the line that hadn't realized that it was hooked! So I had Luke give the line a few firm tugs, and the fish quickly decided to go someplace other than where we were, taking a lot of line in the process.

Luke was excited, convinced he'd hooked a monster. Being fairly strong for a nearly-eight-year old, he planted the pole butt into his midsection, raised the rod tip as much as he could—and hung on! By this time, Dad had cut the motor to idle and was ready to chase the fish. I had reeled in my line to get it out of the way and was focused on helping Luke, who began to play the fish like a pro. Pumping the rod tip and reeling as the fish either rested or swam toward the boat, he began to recover some of the line taken by the fish's initial run.

The fish made another run, this time straight out rather than toward the bottom, and then rolled on the surface about twenty-five yards from the boat. There was no doubt that Luke had hooked a huge King salmon! Dad and I asked him if he was getting tired. "I'm not tired yet!" he responded. "But I will be pretty soon. This fish is strong!"

Three more runs and a little bit of timely help later, Luke had the fish up to the side of the boat. I helped keep the fish's head coming alongside the boat and away from the engine prop while Dad wielded the net, and about twenty-five or thirty minutes after his lunch had been so rudely interrupted, Luke had a massive King salmon in the boat!

As we sat back to rest, we saw Mushroom Rock, a famous landmark of Neah Bay's coastline, a short distance away. Dad smiled at me and asked, "Who could have imagined that your son would catch a thirty-pound King salmon with his dad and grandpa two weeks before his ninth birthday, less than a hundred yards from the exact same spot where you caught a thirty-pound King salmon with me and your grandpa two weeks before your eighth birthday?"

What a nice way to continue a family tradition!

Luke and Grandpa Don with Luke's Thirty-Pound King and Five Cohos

Stan with His Thirty-Pound King

Rabbit Liver Pate with Peach Sauce

Pate Ingredients:

- 2 large or 3 small sweet onions, chopped
- 1 stick butter, divided
- 1 tsp. dried thyme
- 1 lb. rabbit (or chicken) livers, trimmed
- ¼ cup Tawny Port
- ¼ tsp. allspice
- 1 tbsp. lemon juice

Preparation:

1. Cook the onions in 2 tablespoons of the butter in a 12-inch sauté pan over moderate heat, stirring until they are softened. Add the thyme while the onions cook. Set aside to cool, then transfer them to a food processor.
2. In the same pan, melt 2 tablespoons of the remaining butter over moderately high heat until the foam subsides. Pat and dry the chicken livers, then season them with salt and pepper, and sauté them, stirring for 2 minutes, or until they are browned on the outside but still pink inside. Set aside to cool, then transfer them to the food processor.
3. Pour the Port into the same pan, bring it to a boil, and deglaze the skillet, scraping up any brown bits, then remove the pan from the burner and let the Port cool.
4. Add the Port to the food processor with the remaining butter (softened), allspice, lemon juice, and salt and pepper to taste. Purée the mixture until it is smooth and force it through a fine sieve into a bowl.
5. Line a lightly greased 1½-quart terrine or straight-sided dish with plastic wrap and pour in the pâté. Cover and refrigerate for 5 hours or until it is firm. (The pâté may be made up to 4 days in advance and kept covered and chilled).
6. When ready to serve, invert the pâté onto a plate, discarding the plastic wrap, and smooth the top and sides. Pour a small amount of the peach reduction over the top of the pate and serve with toasted baguette slices or water crackers.

Ingredients:

- 2 ripe peaches, halved, with stones removed
- 2 tbsp. margarine
- 1 tbsp. brown sugar
- 1 tsp. cinnamon

Preparation:

1. Bring 1 quart of water to a boil in a 2-quart soup pot. Plunge the peach halves into the boiling water for 1½ to 2 minutes, then transfer them to a bowl of ice water and the skins should slip off easily
2. Cut all 4 halves into ¼-inch cubes.
3. Melt the margarine in a 9-inch sauté pan over medium high heat. Add the peach cubes, the sugar, and the cinnamon; and cook, stirring until tender.
4. Transfer the mixture to a small bowl, spooning some over the pate, leaving the rest to add as needed.

Apple and Raisin Slaw

Ingredients:

- ½ cup golden raisins
- ½ head cabbage, washed, cored, and shredded
- ½ cup Jonagold apple, peeled, cored, and diced
- ¼ cup walnuts, chopped
- 1 tbsp. lemon juice
- ½ cup reduced-fat mayonnaise
- ⅛ cup grated orange rind
- 1 tbsp. orange juice
- ¾ tsp. kosher salt
- ½ tsp. paprika
- ½ tsp. medium grind white pepper
- 1 tsp. sugar

Preparation:

1. Soak the raisins in hot water for 10 minutes, then drain and chill.
2. In a large serving bowl, combine the chilled raisins, cabbage, apples, and walnuts. Cover and chill.
3. In a medium mixing bowl, mix together the lemon juice, mayonnaise, orange rind, orange juice, salt, paprika, pepper, and sugar. Blend thoroughly.
4. Add the dressing mixture to the cabbage, apples, and raisin mixture; and toss thoroughly, then sprinkle with grated orange rind and serve.

Alder SmokeRoasted King Salmon

Since my Dad's first taste of salmon smoked by Native American Indians on the Olympic Peninsula, he wanted to learn firsthand how they catch and cook salmon. After watching, asking lots of questions, and experiencing the process used by the Makah and other local tribes, he learned to replicate their age-old approach each summer while I was growing up. I'll explain the authentic process first, then tell you how to get pretty much the same results with a little less work!

The Authentic Method

The authentic approach involves crafting a two-sided "mesh" in which the fish is suspended over alder coals to roast. To make the mesh and the support stakes, start by cutting twelve to fifteen live alder limbs about one-half- to three-fourth-inch in diameter and about three feet long, and six limbs at least one inch in diameter and about four feet long. Trim the extending leaves and branches from all of the limbs and discard. Both because of their flexibility and because they won't burn, live/green branches are critical!

Lay three of the one-inch diameter branches to make a large V and bind one end of all three together with stout wire or another kind of non-flammable/non-heat-susceptible material. Be sure that the opposite ends of the branches remain spread so that the span is nearly as wide as each fillet is long. Then, using three or four of the smaller branches, "weave" them across the three large branches to form a crude mesh. Bind the smaller branches to the larger branches to make sure that they don't come unraveled. Lay one of the fillets across the mesh, then use three or four of the smaller branches to bind them to the larger branches and the smaller branches as needed and create another weave pattern so that the fillet is held inside the crude "basket."

The Realistic Approach

Cooking

Soak about 3 cups of alder wood chips (available at most home improvement stores) in water for 20 to 30 minutes, then remove to a sheet of paper towels to dry slightly.

Prepare a charcoal fire in a barbeque, letting the coals burn until they are covered with white ash. Spread the coals evenly across the bottom of the barbeque, then add a dozen or so new briquets.

After removing the head, fillet the salmon along each side of the backbone down to the tale. Discard the backbone and rib bones but leave the skin on!

Spread two handfuls of the alder chips over the coals, then place the grill over the coals. Close the barbeque's lid for 5 minutes until smoke begins to curl out of the vents.

Place the fish onto the grill. Sprinkle each fillet with a little kosher salt and fresh ground black pepper then baste them generously with butter as they cook and add a few additional alder chips to the fire now and then if needed to keep the smoke coming.

Depending on how close the fish is to the coals, how hot the coals are, and how thick the fillets are, cooking can take from around fifteen minutes to thirty minutes. Using your (clean) finger, check occasionally for firmness and watch for the juices to run clear. When you think the fish is nearly done cooking, use a spatula that is at least as long as the filet to flip it over gently. Add another handful of alder chips – a few minutes of thick smoke will give the fish a wonderful finish!

Remove the filet gently from the grate onto a platter, garnish with a little fresh parsley or basil, and serve.

Roast Corn on the Cob

Ingredients:

- 4 fresh-picked ears of sweet corn, still in their husks
- 2 tbsp. vegetable oil

Preparation:

1. Brush the husk of each ear of corn with the oil.
2. Place the corn on a metal grate over the charcoal fire, turning every 5 minutes or so. Cook for a total of 14 to 18 minutes, then transfer with oven mitts to a cutting board.
3. Remove the husks, brush each ear with soft butter, and serve immediately.

Suggested Accompaniment

- *Chardonnay:* Chateau St. Michelle Canoe Ridge—Columbia Valley, Washington

Alder Smoke-Roasted King Salmon*
***Sockeye Salmon substituted**

Cold Encounters

I was wearing several layers of wool, but it was the coldest I'd ever been as I stepped from the camper. Four friends and I had travelled from Seattle to the Sinlahekin game management unit near Tonasket, Washington, into nearly a foot of snow and nose-numbing cold to hunt deer for ten days of the late, either sex bow season.

In addition to being a wintering area for both whitetail and mule deer, the Sinlahekin is home to two herds of Rocky Mountain bighorn sheep, one with nearly seventy animals, and the other with about forty animals.

We arrived late Friday afternoon and set up camp in our usual spot just off the road that wound through the valley bottom. The temperature was a balmy thirty-two degrees, but the forecast promised falling temperatures for the balance of our hunt. By Sunday morning, the temperature had fallen to seven degrees as I exited the cozy trailer in the dark.

My hunting buddies, Steve, Larry, Doug, and George, usually preferred to drive several miles up nearby logging roads to ambush deer working along ridge tops looking for sunny slopes on which to bed. I, on the other hand, preferred to spot and stalk or still hunt— climbing the steep hills, flanking the valley in the dark, and positioning myself in draws or thickets as the deer finished their nocturnal feeding and headed up the hills. As the day wore on, I would move to higher vantage points to glass for critters bedded part way up the hill and then stalk them from above.

Although the sun wouldn't lighten the sky for another hour, I could see clearly up and down the valley floor in the moonlight and spotted four different groups of deer as they emerged from foliage that hugged a small stream that paralleled the road. Spotting them was always easier than intercepting them, but being on the hillside before the deer headed back up the hill gave me a little advantage once they committed to their route.

I watched a small group with my 8×30 binoculars as they began to move toward the hillside, then snuck through a small patch of wild rosehips to reposition myself. They picked their way around stubby sagebrush and cheat grass clumps nearly a hundred yards below me as I settled in behind a veil of branches.

Everything looked perfect: the deer, led by a large doe who was closely followed by a buck with three by three antlers, walked toward me, then watched their back-trail for other deer or pursuers. I had an arrow nocked and was confident that I could come to full draw without being detected in my position behind the brush and tree limbs. The small band finally came to within about forty yards when, without warning, all hell broke loose, and they scattered across the hillside.

Watching in disbelief, I wondered what had happened. There was absolutely no wind, I was reasonably well hidden, and I hadn't moved a muscle for several minutes. I carefully scanned the draw in every direction then saw a coyote that had emerged from a thicket, spooking the deer in the process. I'd never had such an urge to find out what coyote tasted like!

I gathered myself and plotted a route up and across the hillside, looking carefully for any of the scattered deer. By this time, I was within a hundred yards or so of the top of the ridge. Although we'd been hunting the Sinlahekin for five years, I'd never made it to the top of the ridge on the eastern flank of the valley. As I crested the ridge, however, I saw a barbed-wire fence line ahead posted with "NO HUNTING!" signs.

I was now nearly two miles from camp, on my own, and the thought of having to drag an animal back by myself—even though most of the way was downhill—didn't appeal to me! So after a short break to snack on half a sandwich and a candy bar while I glassed the slope to the southwest, I decided to start working my way back down the hill to the wooded valley below.

A couple hundred yards later, I picked up a fresh trail in the snow. However, because the snow was so light and powdery, and over two feet deep, I wasn't able to tell exactly what kind of animal had made the tracks. A cold shiver—and not from the temperature—ran down my back as I thought about the mountain lion I had seen two years earlier, but the plowed path looked as though it had been made by two or three deer walking single file.

I snuck forward with my bow and a nocked arrow at the ready, and somehow sensed something ahead. The hillside, which had been sloping gently, fell away over a rock outcropping. Whatever had made the trail had veered to the right of the rocks, but I stayed above the rocks and dropped to my knees as I peered over the edge.

A rare and beautiful sight greeted me. No more than ten yards ahead, four bighorn rams pawed the snow looking for grass. Even though they weren't legal game, I knelt there in the snow and watched them for nearly twenty minutes as I imagined different shot angles and how they would look over my mantle! Eventually, the cold forced me to back away quietly, muttering unkindly that they weren't legal!

Bighorn Sheep – Photo courtesy of Washington Department of Fish & Game

By the time I reached the aspens, low brush and the stream at the bottom of the valley, the temperature had begun to fall. I had seen several deer on my traverse to the valley floor but had not been able to get into bow range.

I had a long walk back to camp ahead of me, but there was still over an hour of shooting light left, and I darn sure wanted to make the most of it!

After about a mile, the tree line running parallel to the road curved away to expose a grassy meadow. I paused to glass ahead and saw two whitetail does grazing at the far end of the glen, seemingly oblivious to the occasional car or truck that crunched along the gravel road.

White-tailed Deer – Photo Courtesy of Washington Department of Fish & Game

As I hid behind a tree to check the wind and devise a plan, the deer fed into the trees. I needed to get into the trees on the far side of the meadow, keeping myself out of sight in the process. There were a few small bushes for cover, and I was able to reach a large boulder about five yards inside the tree line. I knelt behind the rock and scanned the far end of the meadow with my binoculars, happy to see that the two does were heading toward me at a steady walk.

I nocked an arrow and quickly made sure that the tip of my bow wouldn't catch on any limbs as I drew. As if they were on a string, the deer kept coming down the tree line, and it became clear that they would soon pass behind the boulder from my right to left.

As they stepped behind the huge rock, I drew my bow. My heart thumped as the plan came together, but everything was happening so quickly that I didn't have time to get buck fever!

Suddenly, my peep sight was filled with brown fur: the lead doe had stepped out from behind the rock only three yards away! *Thwack!* The arrow passed directly through the deer and buried itself into the large pine tree, causing both deer to turn toward the tree to see what had made the sound as they bolted forward. They ran about thirty yards then turned broadside and snorted at the noisy tree. A few short seconds later, the wounded deer collapsed, the victim of a double lung/heart shot.

Not moving as I watched the deer expire, a million happy thoughts roiled in my tired mind, and I was sure that the cold encounters of that day would keep me warm for a very long time.

Pheasant Sausage with Fig Jam

Ingredients:

- 2 lb. pheasant (or chukar, partridge, quail, or chicken) boneless leg meat, cut
- into ½ to 1-inch chunks
- ½ lb. unsalted pork fat, cut into ½ to 1-inch chunks
- 1 cup yellow onion, peeled and minced
- 2 tbsp. olive oil
- 2 cloves garlic, minced
- ½ bunch cilantro leaves, finely chopped
- 2 tbsp. mild chili powder
- 1 tsp. kosher salt
- 1 tsp. ground cumin
- ½ tsp. ground allspice
- 2 tbsp. oil-packed sundried tomatoes, rinsed and drained, then chopped
- 2 tbsp. lime juice
- 4 feet of hog casing, soaked and rinsed thoroughly

Preparation:

1. Par-freeze the meat and the fat chunks until they are firm to the touch but not frozen.
2. Grind the par-frozen meat and fat through a coarse plate into a large, nonreactive mixing bowl. Add the onion, oil, garlic, cilantro, chili powder, salt, cumin, allspice, tomatoes, and lime juice; and mix thoroughly with your hands. Cover and chill overnight.
3. Slide the rinsed hog casing onto the stuffing tube, then fill the stuffing horn with the meat mixture. Slowly stuff the casing with the meat mixture, taking care not to overstuff it so that you can twist the stuffed casing into links.
4. Once the casing is filled with the meat mixture, tie off one end and twist the tube into 4- or 5-inch links. When you have finished making the links, tie off the other end.
5. Pierce any air pockets with a sterilized needle, then cook by smoking in a charcoal broiler with dampened smoking chips on the coals or in an electric or propane smoker, until the internal temperature registers 150°F.
6. Refrigerate until time to serve, then slice into ½-inch discs, arrange on a platter, and serve with fig jam (recipe follows) and water crackers.

Fig Jam Ingredients:

- ½ cup sugar
- ½ cup water
- 10 to 12 dried figs
- 3 tbsp. brandy or port
- ½ cup filberts, toasted

Preparation:

1. Preheat the oven to 350°F.
2. In a 1-quart saucepan, combine the sugar, water, figs, and brandy (or port) over medium-high heat. Bring the mixture to a boil, reduce the heat, and simmer for 5 minutes, stirring occasionally until the sugar has dissolved completely.
3. Remove the pan from the heat and allow the syrup to cool while you toast the filberts.
4. Spread the filberts on a cookie sheet and cook for 10 to 12 minutes, then remove and let cool.
5. Pour the fig mixture and the filberts into a food processor and pulse until the mixture is smooth and thick. Transfer to an airtight container and refrigerate for at least 24 hours before serving.

Apple, Pear, and Mixed Greens Salad with Smoked Gouda and Toasted Pecans

Ingredients:

- ½ cup apple juice
- 2 tbsp. apple cider vinegar
- 1 tsp. extra-virgin olive oil
- ½ tsp. grey sea salt
- ¼ tsp. coarsely ground black pepper
- 4 cups salad greens (green leaf lettuce, endive, baby spinach, etc.)
- 1 cup seedless grapes, halved
- 1 medium Gala or McIntosh apple, cored and cut into ¼-inch wide wedges
- 1 medium Bartlett or Bosc pear, cored and cut into ¼-inch wide wedges
- ¼ cup shredded smoked Gouda cheese
- ¼ cup pecans, toasted and finely chopped

Preparation:

1. Preheat the oven to 350°F.
2. In a 1-quart saucepan over medium-high heat, bring the apple juice to a boil, then cook until it reduces to about ⅛ cup.
3. Add, stirring with a whisk, the vinegar, oil, salt, and pepper. Remove from the heat and set aside to cool to room temperature.
4. Place the pecans on a cookie sheet and bake for 15 minutes, then transfer them to a cutting board and finely chop them.
5. Combine the greens, grapes, apple, and pear slices in a large bowl, drizzle ½ of the dressing over the top, add ½ of the pecans and grapes, then toss gently. Repeat with the other half of the dressing, pecans, and grapes.
6. Transfer 1 cup of salad mixture to individual serving plates, top with the shredded cheese and serve.

Venison Liver with BaconHerbMushroom Reduction

Ingredients:

- 1 lb. fresh venison liver, cut into 4 to 6 ¼-inch slices
- 2 cups buttermilk (for soaking)
- ½ cup white flour
- ½ tsp. kosher salt
- 1 tsp. coarsely ground black pepper
- 2 tbsp. extra virgin olive oil
- 4 slices smoked bacon, cut into a ¼-inch dice
- 3 cups chopped Vidalia or Walla Walla sweet onion
- 1 tbsp. capers, drained
- 2 tsp. fresh chopped or 1 tsp. dried tarragon
- ½ cup fresh sliced shiitake mushrooms, stems removed
- ¼ cup dry white wine
- ½ cup chicken stock plus ½ cup beef stock, combined
- ¼ cup fat-free sour cream
- 1 tbsp. Dijon mustard

Preparation:

1. Place the sliced liver in a bowl and add buttermilk to cover. Refrigerate for at least 1 hour.
2. Preheat the oven to 150°F.
3. Put the flour into a shallow bowl or a 1-quart ziplock freezer bag. Remove the liver slices from the milk bath and sprinkle each slice with salt and pepper, then place each slice into the bowl or bag and coat with flour. Shake off any loose flour.
4. In a large skillet, heat the oil over medium-high heat. Sauté the liver until the outside is golden brown—about 2½ to 3 minutes on each side for medium rare. Transfer the cooked slices to an ovenproof serving platter, cover loosely with foil, and place the platter in the warmed oven.
5. Pour off all accumulated oil and return the pan to the burner. Add the bacon and cook about 2 minutes, then add the onion and cook until they are just browned and tender, but not limp—about 5 minutes. Stir in the capers, thyme, and mushrooms, then pour in the wine and reduce until the pan is almost dry. Add the stock and reduce about two thirds, then stir in the sour cream and the mustard, plus ¼ teaspoon kosher salt and ¼ teaspoon black pepper. Bring the sauce to a boil and reduce until it thickens.
6. Remove the platter with the liver from the oven, spoon the sauce over the slices, and serve.

Roasted Cauliflower, Garbanzos, and Olives

Ingredients:

- 3 cups (about half a head) cauliflower florets
- ¾ cup Spanish Manzanilla olives, pitted and halved
- ¾ cup Kalamata olives, pitted and halved
- 1½ cups garbanzo beans (aka chick peas), rinsed and drained
- 6 large garlic cloves, coarsely chopped
- 3 tbsp. extra-virgin olive oil
- ¼ tsp. cayenne pepper
- ¼ tsp. kosher salt
- 2 tbsp. flat-leaf (Italian) parsley leaves, washed and drained

Preparation:

1. Preheat the oven to 425°F.
2. Place the cauliflower, olives, garbanzos, and garlic together in a small roasting pan. Drizzle with the oil, then sprinkle the cayenne and salt over everything. Toss to coat.
3. Bake for 10 to 12 minutes, then stir to ensure even cooking. Continue to bake until the cauliflower is crisp-tender and browned—about 25 minutes total time.
4. Transfer to a serving dish, sprinkle with the parsley, and serve.

Suggested Accompaniment

- *Merlot:* 14 Hands—Columbia Valley, Washington, or Concannon Reserve—Livermore Valley, California

Venison Liver with Bacon/Herb/Mushroom Sauce

Bit by a Blacktail

The day after Thanksgiving in 1992, a neighborhood friend, Rick, his son Chris, and I headed to the western slopes of the Cascade Mountains in Washington near the small logging town of Morton for the late-season bow-hunting season for blacktail deer. The weather forecast was indecisive, but that wasn't at all unusual for western Washington in late November; and we always wore layers of wool to avoid becoming soaked in the cold, wet underbrush.

Departing after a full day's work, we had a two-hour drive to reach an abandoned gravel pit where we would park Rick's camper for the weekend. Fortunately, the traffic was fairly light until we reached Tacoma; but once we got through that mess, it was smooth sailing.

We arose the next morning to a light rain, with the promise of improvement during the day. It had rained the night before, though, so we would be hunting in wet, dense foliage and along abandoned logging roads; so there was no doubt that we would be wet in no time.

Solo hunting is the best way to hunt blacktails. They are most comfortable in the thick undergrowth that grows quickly after an area is logged of its harvestable trees, leaving thick groundcover for the wary deer.

As we bolted down a quick cup of hot coffee and a bowl of oatmeal, we agreed on a plan that would drop me off along the side of a logging road bordered by a thick forest of Douglas firs, red cedars, and salal—also known as Oregon grape. The evergreen shrub blankets the ground throughout much of Western Washington and

Oregon and seems to attract and hold rain drops until a hunter walks by. I was soaked from the waist down in minutes.

I stepped into the forest and started a slow, quiet traverse up and across a hillside, scanning with both my eyes and my binoculars for any sign of movement. It was clear that there were lots of deer in the area, as well used game trails crisscrossed everywhere. I spotted a couple of does ahead to my right, and I fully intended to let an arrow fly if one presented itself!

I crept slowly and quietly through the salal, ducking behind trees often, but it quickly became clear that I was not going to be able to sneak up on them. I watched them as they made their way across the hill toward a large clear cut to my left where they would probably bed down.

I eventually reached the edge of the forest where it opened onto the clear cut that dropped from the ridge back down to the logging road up which we had driven that morning. It was covered by waist- and chest-deep grass and vines between widely spaced young firs. Any shot opportunity would, because of this jungle, be quick and close, and the odds favored the deer!

As I rested and ate lunch. I could see Mt. St. Helens to the east. The mountain—a "dormant" volcano—had erupted in 1981, blowing off the top thousand feet or more of its former profile and spewing ash fifty thousand feet in the air. Now much of the forests and hillsides that had been wiped clean by the blast were covered in new growth that provided food and shelter for a wide variety of wildlife that inhabits the area.

Rising from my perch on the stump of a harvested fir tree, I made my way into the underbrush, vines, and trees. I quickly found that I would have to stop every few yards to re-center my hat and face mask because the brush was grabbing and turning them so that I couldn't see out of the mask! By three o'clock, I was about two thirds of the way down the hill toward the logging road. I had seen the rumps and tails of two deer but had not managed to get a shot at them.

Just as I stopped to adjust my hat and face mask—again—a slight movement twenty yards straight down the hill caught my eye. Because of the close-and-quick shot situation, I kept an arrow nocked at all times; so when I saw the movement, I instinctively raised the bow into shooting position. I came to full draw as a large doe rose from the grass beside a fir tree. Much to my frustration, my facemask had been pulled off-center by the brush so that the eye holes weren't aligned with my eyes, and my sight picture through the peephole sight on my bowstring was a double image! I knew that if I let down to straighten the mask, the deer would be gone in an instant, so I put the twenty-yard sight pin on the deer's chest—or was that its head— and released the arrow.

Thwack! The arrow hit the deer squarely between the eyes and she crumpled to the ground. I didn't know whether to curse or thank my facemask for "screwing up" my shot: no one would intentionally try to shoot a deer in the forehead at twenty yards!

As I bent over the deer, I saw that the broadhead had buried itself in the back of the skull. I was not able to work it free without breaking the broadhead and/or the arrow, so I unscrewed the arrow from the broadhead and ran my fingers across the back of the deer's head to confirm that the blade was not exposed.

After field dressing my trophy and dragging her over fallen logs and through brambles for nearly a hundred yards, I found a large rock on the side of the road on which I could sit and wait for Rick and Chris to pick me up. They arrived a half hour later, and we hoisted my harvest into the camper and made the short drive back to camp to dress and skin it.

By the time we pulled into our campsite, everyone was ready for dinner, so we had to get the deer out of the camper. Rick grabbed the hind legs and I grabbed the front legs, tucking the head up between the front legs. Everything went smoothly until I stepped down from the main floor of the camper onto the bumper. As I lifted the deer to clear the bumper, the head slipped between the legs and slid down my pants leg. Although I didn't feel any real pain, I instantly knew something was wrong.

"Stop!" I shouted to Rick.

"What?" he replied.

"My leg feels funny," I said.

"Let's finish getting the deer to the ground," he suggested, knowing that we needed the deer out of the way in any event.

After lowering the deer to the ground, we stepped back into the camper. Rick knelt down to look at my leg and quickly saw that the pant leg was sliced open and that I had a six-inch gash running down the inside of my right shin bone! Rick had a spectacular first-aid kit in the camper, and Chris, an Eagle Scout, immediately began taping me up.

"That damn deer bit me!" I said, laughing, as Chris wrapped my leg. Fortunately, the "bite"—which we later confirmed was made by the broadhead protruding a mere quarter inch from the back of the deer's head—was shallow and 'clean,' so there was very little blood.

Despite my strenuous objections, Rick and Chris insisted that we drive into town to have the cut looked at. Almost two hours later, with seventeen shiny, new stitches in my leg, Rick made the decision to wrap up the hunt for that weekend and head home.

Crunchy Bean Sprout Salad

Ingredients:

- ¼ cup vegetable oil
- 2 tbsp. rice wine vinegar
- 1 tbsp. sesame oil
- 1 tsp. chili-flavored oil
- ¼ cup shiitake mushrooms, stems removed and cut
- into ¼-inch slices
- 2 medium carrots, washed, peeled, and shredded
- 1 small seedless cucumber, washed, peeled, and coarsely chopped
- ½ cup bean sprouts
- ¼ cup fresh snow pea pods, washed and drained, then cut into ¼-inch strips
- 4 radicchio leaves, washed, drained and trimmed
- 1 cup Chinese noodles
- 4 tsp. toasted sesame seeds, divided

Preparation:

1. In a small mixing bowl, combine the vegetable oil, vinegar, sesame oil, and chili oil and stir with a whisk until thoroughly blended.
2. Put the mushrooms in a large mixing bowl, add the oil mixture, and toss gently to coat evenly.
3. Place a radicchio leaf on individual salad plates and spoon the vegetable mixture onto each leaf. Sprinkle each salad with Chinese noodles and sesame seeds before serving.

Braised Blacktail Saddle Roast

My favorite way to process venison—especially smaller, younger animals—is to remove the legs, then make "saddle roasts" by cutting the ribs from the body about five or six inches below and parallel to the backbone and cutting the carcass crosswise every six to eight inches. The result is seven or eight two-sided roasts of backstrap meat—the flavor of which is enhanced by cooking on the bone.

Meat preparation

Several hours before cooking time, rinse the saddle roast and shake the water from it, but do not pat it dry. After it has sat for a few minutes, marinate it until it's time to cook.

Marinade Ingredients:

- 2 tbsp. extra-virgin olive oil
- 2 cloves minced garlic
- 1 cup chicken stock
- ½ cup diced sweet (Vidalia or Walla Walla) onion
- kosher salt and coarsely ground black pepper to taste

Preparation:

1. Mix the ingredients thoroughly in a large, nonreactive bowl. Place the roast into the bag or the bowl, then roll it with your fingers to make sure it's thoroughly coated with the marinade. Refrigerate until cooking time, rotating the roast a couple of times.

Roasting Ingredients:

- 1 cup extra-virgin olive oil
- 1 cup Marsala wine
- 1 tbsp. coarsely ground juniper berries
- 1 tbsp. fresh, coarsely chopped sage leaves (or ½ tbsp. dried, chopped sage leaves)

Preparation:

1. In a large, heavy-bottomed stock pan, over medium heat, heat the oil until shimmering
2. Add to garlic and sauté until it starts to turn brown (about 3 or 4 minutes)
3. Place the roast, meat side down, in the pan and brown for about 3 minutes; rotate to the other side—meat down— and repeat.

- 1 tbsp. kosher or sea salt
- 1 tbsp. coarsely ground black pepper
- ½ tbsp. dried French thyme
- ½ cup sour cream
- 1 tbsp. cornstarch
- ¼ cup cold water

4. Flip the roast over so that it's sitting on the ribs, meat and backbone up, and add the chicken stock. Raise the heat to high to bring the broth to a boil, then flip the roast over—meat and backbone down—and reduce the heat to medium low. Cover, and simmer for 15–20 minutes until a meat thermometer registers 1350 in the center of one of the backstrap sections.
5. Remove the roast from the pan to a plate and cover loosely with foil.
6. Raise the heat to bring the remaining liquid to a boil, then add the sour cream to the sauce and stir, removing any bits stuck to the bottom, until the liquid is fully blended and reduced by about a third.
7. Mix the cornstarch and the cold water together in a small bowl and stir until completely integrated, then add to the sauce and stir until the sauce thickens.
8. Transfer the roast to a serving platter and pour a small amount of the sauce over the meat, reserving the rest for the table.

Roasted Fingerling Potatoes with Dijon Dressing

Ingredients:

- 1½ lb. multicolored fingerling potatoes, washed and drained
- 1 tsp. extra-virgin olive oil
- ¼ tsp. kosher salt
- 1 tbsp. coarsely ground black pepper
- 2 tbsp. honey mustard
- 1½ tbsp. honey
- 1 tbsp. fresh chives, chopped

Preparation:

1. Pre-heat the oven to 425°F.
2. Place the potatoes in a single layer in a 9×12-inch lightly greased casserole dish, then brush each potato with oil, salt, and pepper. Cook until golden brown and tender—about 30 minutes, stirring them once during cooking.
3. While the potatoes are cooking, blend the mustard, honey, and chives together in a small mixing bowl.
4. When the potatoes are done, remove them from the oven and allow them to cool for a few minutes, then coat with the honey mixture, toss gently, and serve.

Sauted Brussels Sprouts

Ingredients:

- 24 small brussels sprouts, washed and trimmed, with torn or "raggy" outer leaves removed, and halved vertically
- 1 tbsp. extra-virgin olive oil, plus 1 tbsp.
- kosher salt and coarsely ground black pepper, to taste
- 1/4 cup grated parmesan cheese

Preparation:

1. Gently rub each sprout half with olive oil, being careful not to break it into pieces.
2. Heat 1 tablespoon of olive oil in a large sauté pan over medium heat. Don't overheat the oil, or the sprouts will cook too quickly.
3. Place the sprout halves in the pan, flat side down (single layer), sprinkle lightly with salt and pepper, then cover and cook for about 5 minutes until the bottoms of the sprouts show a hint of browning. Remove one-half and cut it open to determine whether they're tender throughout; cover and cook for a few more minutes if needed.
4. Once the sprouts reach the desired tenderness, remove the pan lid and turn up the heat, then cook until the flat sides are seared and caramelized. Toss them once or twice to get some browning on the rounded side.
5. Season with a little more salt and a dusting of grated cheese, and toss gently until the cheese melts, then serve immediately.

Suggested Accompaniment

- *Petite Syrah:* Bogle—Clarksburg, California, or Ravenswood—Woodbridge, California
- *Zinfandel:* James Creek Vineyards—St. Helena, California, or Campus Oaks—Lodi, California

Braised Black-tail Deer Saddle Roast

Trout for a Trio

When my father called to invite me and my son Luke to go trout fishing, we were both excited. We weren't familiar with Douglas Lake Ranch, but fishing in the Canadian Okanogan Valley sounded promising, especially since we would be one of the first guests at the ranch that spring—not long after the winter snow and ice melted from the landscape and the lake's surfaces.

As we prepared for the trip, Dad asked a friend of his who had fished at the ranch what kinds of flies would work. The answer was "Wooly Buggers, in black, black or silver, red, and green, on long shanked size 6 or 4 hooks." Any trout that eats bugs that big is big too! Ever the traditionalist, but with fifty years of experience to back it up, Dad added several variations on his Self-Bodied Carey pattern—an ugly fly with a body of brown or greenish ringnecked pheasant rump feathers, a scraggly hackle of slightly lighter colored rump feathers, and a black head.

We drove from Seattle to the Canadian border north of Blaine, Washington, then northeast through the mountains. After a bathroom and gas break in the lonely little wind-swept town of Merritt, British Columbia, we pushed onward, hoping to reach the ranch early enough to fish a little before nightfall. After we checked in at the main lodge, one of the ranch hands led us to our "cabin." We had imagined a small one- or two-roomed shack with an outhouse and were pleasantly surprised that it was nothing short of a log mansion with a five-star kitchen!

We still had about two hours left before dark, so we grabbed our rods and other gear, and making darned sure to dress warmly, walked from the cabin to the edge of the lake. I helped load Luke's gear into the first boat we reached while Dad tied Wooly Buggers—Luke's red and Dad's green—to their lines.

It took a couple of runs up and down the shorelines, fighting the cold breeze as we went, to determine that the fish were at a depth of fifteen to twenty feet. We also learned that red with added shiny Mylar strands was their color of choice.

With our hands and fingers smarting from the cold wind, we weren't sorry when darkness drove us from the lake. Returning to the welcoming light and warmth of the cabin, Dad and I sipped on a single-malt scotch while I prepared dinner.

The next morning broke clear and cool, and the wind had quieted. Dad was in the kitchen fixing breakfast when I came downstairs. Luke wasn't up yet, but the smell of bacon and eggs would have him up and about before long!

Over coffee, Dad and I agreed to try Big Minnie Lake, where his friend had always done well in the early season. We packed lunch, a thermos of coffee and some sodas, grabbed our rods and gear, and headed out the door.

It wasn't long before Luke and Dad were playing a fish, so I decided to row in their direction. I saw that Luke had a very nice fish hooked and was doing a great job playing it. It took short but strong dives, stripping line as it went; and he would work it back toward the boat with firm but gentle pressure, hand-stripping the line rather than playing it on the reel. Having only a two-pound test leader, Luke knew that he needed to be careful to keep the fish from breaking off.

Finally, after a fifteen-minute battle, Luke brought the beautiful rainbow trout alongside the boat and his grandpa netted it.

"It's twenty-one inches," Luke said as he gently measured the fish. "That's my biggest trout ever, Grandpa!"

"Let's get a picture," Dad replied as he pulled his camera from his gear bag.

We explored different areas of the lake for the next two hours, getting a few strikes here and there, hooking up about every third time, and catching brightly colored rainbows ranging from fourteen to seventeen inches. The temperature rose gradually, and even with a slight breeze from the southwest, we had a comfortable lunch in the sun as we watched a pair of Osprey searching for fish near the surface in a shallow cove. A few minutes after we started watching them, the female dove straight into the water but came flapping back to the surface "empty-handed." We continued to watch the graceful birds for another half hour before deciding that it was time to get back out onto the lake.

Soon after rounding the point of land protecting the Osprey's hunting area, Dad hooked into a nice fish.

"Dad," I shouted, "keep an eye on that Osprey. He wants your fish!"

"I noticed," Dad grinned back. "But the fish wants to go deep rather than stay on the surface." Dad soon had the hefty twenty-three-inch fish tuckered out, and Luke brought it into the boat for him.

I also managed to hook and boat a few fish that day—the largest of which was a very chubby nineteen-inch hen. We fished until dark before heading back to the cabin for steaks on the barbeque and a couple of games of gin rummy. As we had the night before, we all slept very well indeed!

Stoney Lake was our destination the next morning, but we were only able to scare up a couple of small fish over three hours and decided to head back to the cabin and fish Little Minnie Lake for the rest of the afternoon. The result was the same as it had been the first night: a few strikes, a few hookups, but no fish of any size. We tried different rowing speeds and different depths, and switched flies frequently, but nothing seemed to help.

I asked Dad if he had any "leech" flies, thinking that anything was worth a try. He dug into his gear bag for his box of wet flies and streamers, and pulled out a fly with a black, 2-inch strip of rabbit fur, and a hot-pink head. I quickly tied it onto my leader, set my line at a depth of about fifteen feet, and started rowing slowly down the shoreline.

Within moments, a fish struck the leech, jerking the rod tip into the water. Dad and Luke watched as I boated and released a nice "little" eighteen-inch fish and hooked another fish a few minutes later.

"Leech patterns for everyone!" Dad said as he and Luke retrieved their lines and changed flies. They both too quickly hooked fish, and although none of us managed to catch anything over eighteen inches, we had a blast until darkness pushed us off the lake.

The next day, on our long drive home, we recounted our adventure and agreed that we'd caught plenty of trout for a trio!

SheCrab Soup

Ingredients:

- ¼ lb. butter or margarine
- ¾ cup flour
- 1 cup fat-free Half-and-Half or fat-free sour cream
- 3 cups milk
- 2 cups chicken soup base
- ¼ lb. crab roe (if available)
- 1 lb. lump or blue crab meat
- ½ cup chopped celery
- ¼ cup chopped carrots
- ¼ cup chopped onion
- ¼ cup sherry, plus ¼ tsp. per serving bowl, divided
- ½ tsp. Tabasco sauce
- 1 tbsp. Worcestershire sauce
- 4 tsp. fat-free sour cream, divided
- 1 tsp. sherry, divided

Preparation:

1. Melt butter or margarine in a 4-quart stockpot over medium-low heat.
2. Stir in the flour to make a roux, then add the Half-and-Half or sour cream and milk, and slowly bring it to a boil.
3. Add the chicken soup base, crab roe and meat, celery, carrots, onion, sherry, Tabasco and Worcestershire sauces, and reduce the heat to medium low.
4. Simmer for 20 minutes, garnish each bowl with a dollop of sour cream and ¼ teaspoon of sherry.

Peaches with Sliced Almonds and Raisins

Ingredients:

- 4 ripe peaches, washed, blanched, peeled, and halved, stones removed
- ½ cup raisins
- 2 tbsp. lemon juice
- 2 tbsp. sugar
- ¼ tsp. almond extract
- ½ cup sliced or chopped almonds

Preparation:

1. Blanch the peaches by placing them in a medium saucepot of boiling water for 30 seconds. Transfer them to a work surface and let rest a few minutes until cool enough to handle. Halve each peach vertically, then slip off the peel and remove the stone.
2. Cut the peach halves vertically into
3. ½-inch slices, transfer to a large bowl and add the raisins. Chill for 30 minutes.
4. In a small bowl, blend the lemon juice and sugar, stirring until the sugar dissolves.
5. Pour the mixture over the peaches and raisins, add the almond extract, and toss gently to coat thoroughly.
6. Transfer to individual compote cups and sprinkle with almonds before serving.

Smoked Rainbow Trout over Artichoke Heart Salad with Feta Cheese Vinaigrette

Ingredients:

- 8 rainbow trout fillets, with skin on
- 1 qt. very warm (but not hot) water
- 1½ cups white sugar
- 1 tsp. dried, crushed thyme, plus ½ tsp.
- 4 tbsp. kosher salt

Preparation:

1. In a 6-quart nonreactive bowl, mix the sugar, 1 teaspoon of thyme, and the salt into the warm water. Immerse the fillets in the solution, then cover with a lid or plastic wrap, and refrigerate overnight.

2. Remove the fillets from the pan after 16 to 20 hours, rinse under cold water to remove all of the mixture, and pat dry. After about an hour, the fillets will develop a sticky glaze called the "pellicle"; at which time, they are ready for smoking.

3. Light a charcoal fire of 10 to 12 briquettes in an aluminum pie plate with several small holes in the bottom. Separately, plunge about 3 cups of hardwood smoking chips into a bucket of water for five minutes, then remove them to a flat surface to drain and dry.

4. Place the fillets on a narrow-grooved barbeque grate sprayed with non-stick spray, and sprinkle the extra ½ teaspoon thyme lightly over the fillets.

5. Once the briquettes have a thin coating of white ash on them, spread them evenly in the pie tin using a metal poker or green stick. Place a small handful of the wood chips directly onto the hot coals, then place the grate with the fillets into the barbeque as far away from the charcoal as possible. Close the lid on the barbeque.

6. About every 30 minutes, open the lid of the barbeque and "stir" the coals gently to allow them to get some oxygen. Add another small handful of wood chips and reclose the barbeque lid.

7. When the fish has a smoky finish and is slightly firm to the touch, remove the grate from the barbeque, and then remove the fish from the grate.

Artichoke Heart Salad with Feta Cheese Vinaigrette

Ingredients:

- ¼ cup rice vinegar
- 1 tsp. fresh basil, minced
- 1 tsp. fresh dill, minced
- 1 tsp. fresh mint, minced
- ½ cup olive oil
- ¼ cup safflower oil
- 1 tsp. sugar
- kosher salt and coarsely ground black pepper, to taste
- 2 cups (one 16-oz. jar or can) of artichoke hearts packed in water, quartered
- 1 beefsteak tomato, washed and cored, then cut into ½-inch cubes

Preparation:

1. Whisk the vinegar, herbs, and cheese together in a small mixing bowl.
2. Add the olive and safflower oils in a slow thin stream, whisking constantly. Stir in the sugar and whisk until all of the ingredients are thoroughly combined and thoroughly blended.
3. Season to taste with salt and pepper, then set aside until ready to use.
4. Mix the artichoke hearts and the tomatoes together in a large mixing bowl, and add the dressing and toss gently.
5. Arrange a serving of salad on each plate and top with chunks of the smoked trout

Country Cornbread

Ingredients:

- 2 cups stone-ground cornmeal
- 1 cup all-purpose flour
- 2½ tsp. baking powder
- ½ tsp. baking soda
- ¾ tsp. salt
- 2 large eggs
- ¾ cup buttermilk
- ¾ cup milk
- 3 tbsp. honey
- ¼ cup melted butter, slightly cooled

Preparation:

1. Pre-heat the oven to 400°F.
2. Spray a 9-inch square baking pan with non-stick cooking spray.
3. Combine the cornmeal, flour, baking powder, soda, and salt in a large mixing bowl and blend thoroughly.
4. In a separate mixing bowl, whisk together the eggs, buttermilk, milk, honey, and melted butter.
5. Stir the egg mixture into the dry mixture until blended thoroughly, then pour the combined mixture into the prepared baking pan.
6. Bake for 25 to 35 minutes, or until the top is a light, golden brown. Cool and serve.

Suggested Accompaniment

- *Chardonnay:* Rex Goliath—Acampo, California

Smoked Trout over Artichoke Heart Salad with Feta Vinaigrette

Mostly Mallards

In late December 1995, my work colleague and friend, Steve, invited me and my fourteen-year-old son, Luke, to go duck hunting with him and his father, Sam, near Moses Lake, Washington. We knew the weather might be nasty, but we headed eastward on December 27 in high spirits.

Luke and I drove cautiously over Snoqualmie Pass and past Ellensburg, then crossed the Columbia River and veered north to Steve's hunting club. After the long drive, we were anxious to see how Steve and Sam had done earlier that day.

Steve had a forty-foot mobile home outfitted with running water and propane for heat and cooking, and he insisted that we bunk there. We were only going to be there two nights, so we had packed lightly and transferred everything from the car in short order.

As we worked, Steve said that the hunting had been mediocre so far, but that things should pick up the next day. He knew that Luke had never hunted ducks before and that he was anxious to go out that afternoon, so he offered to take us out before dark. I grabbed Luke's 20-gauge side-by-side and my 12-gauge side-by-side, along with our ammo, and loaded them into the truck next to several sacks of decoys. Finally, we loaded Steve's chocolate lab, Rosie, into her crate in the back and headed out.

Since time was limited, Steve drove us to a small, shallow pond on the far side of the property that was close to several harvested cornfields in which the ducks fed during the day, and he knew that we could set out two dozen decoys very quickly in the pond's shallow water. Once the decoys were in place, we positioned ourselves in blinds on either side of the south end of the pond.

Ducks had already started to fly into the cornfields to feed, so Steve began calling to several small flocks flying toward the fields. It wasn't long before one of the groups took interest in our spread and veered toward the pond. As we watched them set their wings and begin to glide toward us, I told Luke that he could shoot first.

Luke took aim and fired twice. A beautiful drake mallard crashed into the pond. "That's my first duck!" he exclaimed. "Can we get it mounted?"

"You'll have plenty of other opportunities to kill ducks. Let's not get carried away!" I replied.

An hour and several downed ducks later, a small flock approached. I rose from my seat and took aim at the lead drake, hoping that I was leading him enough, and was relieved when the bird folded. Rosie was on it within seconds, and when she had returned it to Steve, he called out, "You just shot a redhead!"

"Is that bad?" I yelled back. "They aren't protected, are they?"

"No," he replied. "We just don't see very many around here!"

By the time we headed back to the club for dinner, we had bagged seven ducks. Luke and I, not accustomed to having to pick out the drakes, had each shot a hen, but the remaining five birds were drakes.

We arose early the next morning to a brisk wind and a couple inches of snow, but Steve was encouraged by the change, figuring that any flocks to our north would stop to eat in the club's fields. Sam suggested that we put out a few goose decoys as well.

"I'm way ahead of you, Dad," Steve responded as he dropped the last few of a dozen goosed decoys into the truck bed.

After a short drive, we quickly unloaded the decoys at the edge of a reedy marsh. Steve explained that there were two metal box blinds sunk into the mud in six inches of water and surrounded by cattails about thirty yards from shore. He headed for a blind that had a platform for Rosie behind it, and waved Luke and me to the other. Before we started to follow, however, Sam said that he didn't want to climb down into the sunken boxes and offered to take Luke and a few decoys to a box blind further up the slough. We wished them luck and settled into our blinds.

Once there was enough light, we saw ducks everywhere! Several mallards swam nervously to our right, and a larger flock paddled upstream to our left. We didn't need decoys—we had live volunteers!

When legal shooting time arrived, Steve began his quack-chatter calling sequences. It didn't take long for several birds to come in, and Steve and I quickly had our first birds down.

A few minutes later, I spotted a group of birds coming in from our left and immediately started mouth calling. Steve watched in amazement as the birds circled our decoy spread, and we soon downed three handsome drakes. He later said that he'd been calling ducks for more than twenty years and had never seen anyone call them in by mouth.

We were also happy to hear shots ringing out from where Sam and Luke were hunting, but by nine thirty, there weren't any more birds flying, so we decided to head in. Between us, we had killed nine birds, including a blue-winged teal and a nice male shoveler. After packing up the decoys, we sat on a small mound to wait for

Sam and Luke, but we didn't have to wait long before they came bouncing down the road toward us.

"How'd you guys do?" Steve asked Luke as he climbed out of the truck.

"I think we got seven birds, didn't we, Mr. Phillips?" Luke replied.
"Yep. Luke made some pretty good shots too!" Sam said.

After loading Rosie, the decoys, and our gear into the truck, we were all glad to be in the warmth of the truck's cabin. The outside temperature had dropped steadily throughout the morning and was hovering around thirty degrees. Fortunately, though, it had stopped snowing for the time being!

Once we were back at the trailer, we grabbed the ducks and headed for the club's processing room. There were large metalwork tables and sinks arranged in a brightly lit room to expedite the process, and since Luke had never cleaned a duck, I was happy to give him his first lesson.

Once the birds were cleaned, plucked, and freezer-bagged, we headed back to the trailer for a hot shower and brunch. We had forgotten how hungry we were and quickly set about wolfing down the large platter of bacon, eggs, and toast Sam had prepared for us.

The weather report on the television was advising motorists that several inches of snow would likely fall in the passes that night, so Steve suggested that we take the birds we had all killed and head home.

Reluctantly, Luke and I quickly loaded up our gear, thanked Steve and his dad for a great hunt, then over the river and through the trees to grandmother's house we went, with memories of a fun hunt and a cooler full of "mostly mallards" to show for it!

Duck Breast Prosciutto

Ingredients:

- 2 8-oz. duck breasts, rinsed and patted dry
- ½ cup sea (or kosher) salt
- 1 cup brown sugar
- 2 tbsp. fennel seeds
- 2 tbsp. ground mace
- 2 tbsp. pickling spices
- 2 tbsp. fresh rosemary, coarsely chopped
- 2 tbsp. fresh thyme
- 2 tbsp. fresh sage leaves, coarsely chopped
- cheesecloth
- butcher's twine

Preparation:

1. Score both sides of each breast about 1/8-inch deep in a diamond pattern.
2. Combine the salt, brown sugar, fennel seeds, and mace in a mixing bowl.
3. Massage the mixture into each breast, place them in the refrigerator on a nonreactive covered plate overnight, and remove and brush off any excess salt.
4. Cut two pieces of cheesecloth (double thickness) large enough to wrap each breast.
5. Mix the herbs in a small mixing bowl, then divide the mixture into 4 equal portions. Spread a portion over the surface of each breast, flip each breast, and spread the remaining 2 portions over the surface of each breast.
6. Place each breast on one of the cheesecloth pieces and wrap it, covering completely, then bind into a packet with the twine, leaving a long piece of twine on each.
7. Hang the bundles in a cool, dry place for 2 weeks. Test for doneness by squeezing the meat gently. When it is firm, with no give, remove it from the cheesecloth.

Bib Lettuce and Red Onion Salad with Raspberry Balsamic Vinaigrette

Ingredients:

- ½ cup extra-virgin olive oil
- ½ cup raspberry balsamic vinegar
- 1 clove garlic, minced
- 1 tsp. ground mustard
- ½ tsp. dried thyme
- kosher salt and coarsely ground black pepper, to taste
- 3 cups bib lettuce leaves, washed and drained
- ½ red onion, peeled and cut crosswise into thin slices

Preparation:

1. In a small mixing bowl, whisk together olive oil, white balsamic vinegar, garlic, and mustard powder. Season to taste with salt and black pepper. Chill in the refrigerator before serving.
2. Arrange the lettuce leaves on individual serving plates and top with a few onion slices.
3. Drizzle about 1 teaspoon of the dressing over each plate, reserving the rest for the table.

Green Beans with Basil Pesto

Ingredients:

- 4 garlic cloves, peeled
- 2 cups fresh basil leaves, washed and drained, then coarsely chopped
- 1 cup grated Asiago cheese
- ¾ cup extra-virgin olive oil, divided
- kosher salt and coarsely ground black pepper, to taste
- 1 lb. green bush beans, washed, drained and trimmed
- ¼ cup toasted pine nuts

Preparation:

1. Place the garlic, basil cheese, 3 tablespoons of the oil, salt and pepper in a food processor and puree to make a paste.
2. With the motor running, pour the remaining oil into the processor in a slow stream. Set aside.
3. Preheat the oven to 350°F.
4. Fill a 2-quart saucepan with a steamer rack with enough water to reach the bottom of the steamer and bring the water to a boil, then add the beans, and cook until they are tender—about 4 minutes.
5. While the water is boiling and the beans are cooking, place the pine nuts on a cookie sheet and cook in the oven for 8 minutes.
6. Transfer the beans and the pesto to a medium mixing bowl, toss gently, then transfer to a serving dish. Sprinkle the warm pine nuts over the top and serve.

OvenRoasted Wild Duck

Ingredients:

- 2 whole ducks, cleaned and plucked (skin on, with shot pellets removed)
- cooking spray
- ½ cup coarsely chopped fresh rosemary or sage leaves
- 2 small yellow onions, cut vertically in 1/8 sections
- 1 cup chicken soup base
- kosher or coarse sea salt, to taste
- coarsely ground black pepper, to taste

Preparation:

1. Pre-heat the oven to 400°F.
2. Place a roasting rack inside a roasting pan and coat both the rack and the pan with the cooking spray.
3. Lay the ducks breast side up on a clean, flat surface. With your fingers, gently push a tablespoon of the chopped rosemary or sage under the skin from the body cavity toward the head. Repeat on the other side of the body. Repeat from the head toward the body cavity on both sides. Repeat the entire process on the other duck.
4. Stuff the body cavity of each duck with a sectioned onion, then place both ducks, breast-side up, on the roasting rack. Apply a light coating of cooking spray to each duck, sprinkle with salt and pepper to taste, and cover both ducks loosely with aluminum foil.
5. Pour the chicken soup base into the bottom of the roasting pan, place the roasting rack in the pan, then insert a meat thermometer into the smaller of the two ducks so that the tip is in the thickest part of the breast.
6. Roast the ducks, basting and checking the meat thermometer occasionally, until the meat thermometer registers 125°F—about 55 to 60 minutes. Remove the foil and baste the ducks with the soup base and accumulated juices, then return the roasting pan to the oven.
7. When the thermometer registers 140°F, remove the roasting pan from the oven. Transfer both ducks to a serving platter and serve with wild rice pilaf.

Roasted Tomatoes with Wild Rice and Anchovies

Ingredients:

- 2 beefsteak tomatoes, washed and drained then cut in half crosswise
- 3 cups water
- 1 cup wild rice
- kosher salt and coarsely ground black pepper, to taste
- 1 tbsp. Tarragon vinegar
- 1 tsp. red wine vinegar
- 1 scallion, washed, drained and cut into ½-inch slices
- 6 (oil-packed) anchovy fillets, minced
- ¼ cup fresh flat-leaf (Italian) parsley, washed and drained, then coarsely chopped, plus 2 whole sprigs
- 3 tbsp. extra-virgin olive oil

Preparation:

1. Preheat the oven to 400°F.
2. Place the tomato halves on a cookie sheet, cut side down, and roast for 12 minutes, or until the skin begins to wrinkle. Remove from the oven and transfer to a cutting board. Let cool enough to handle, then remove the skins and chop coarsely. Set aside.
3. Heat the water in a 1-quart saucepan to a boil. Stir in the rice with a little salt and pepper, return to a boil, then reduce the heat to low and cover until the rice has absorbed the water—about 25 minutes. Remove from the heat and let it stand, covered, for another 15 minutes.
4. Transfer the rice to a bowl and add the vinegars, onion, anchovies, parsley, and 3½ to 4 tablespoons of oil, plus all but 2 tablespoons of the tomatoes, and a little salt and pepper. Toss gently to mix thoroughly.
5. Transfer the mixture to a serving bowl and garnish with the remaining tomato pieces and parsley sprigs. Serve immediately.

Tomato, Duck Prosciutto, and Blue Cheese on Toasts

Ingredients:

- 8 slices of baguette bread ½-inch thick
- 2 tbsp. extra-virgin olive oil
- 2 cloves garlic, minced
- 1 tsp. dry sherry
- 8 slices of duck prosciutto (about the same size
- as the bread slices)
- 8 Roma tomato slices
- ¼- to ½-inch thick
- kosher salt to taste
- 8 slices of blue cheese
- ¼- to ½-inch thick
- freshly ground pepper
- sweet paprika

Preparation:

1. Preheat the oven to 400°.
2. Brush the tops and bottoms of each bread slice with olive oil and transfer to a baking sheet. Toast for 10 to 15 minutes, turning once, until golden and crisp but still soft inside. Combine the garlic with the sherry in a small bowl, then brush the top of each toast with the mixture.
3. Top each piece of bread with the prosciutto and tomato, season lightly with salt, and top with the cheese.
4. Preheat the broiler. Broil the sandwiches as close to the heat as possible for about 3 minutes, shifting the pan occasionally, until the cheese is bubbling. Sprinkle with pepper and paprika and serve hot.

Suggested Accompaniment

- *Pinot Noir:* Jill's Vineyard—New Zealand or Erath Vineyards—Eugene, Oregon

Roast Wild Duck*
***Domestic duck substituted**

Montana Monarch

In 2001, my friend Mike, the owner and head guide of High Plains Drifter—a fly-fishing outfitting service out of Missoula—suggested that I apply for both a Montana bighorn sheep tag and a pronghorn antelope tag in early 2001.

On September 3, my birthday, I received an envelope from the Montana Fish and Game Department. I was mightily disappointed when I learned that I hadn't drawn a sheep tag, but got over it quickly as I fingered an antelope tag.

The area in which we'd be hunting had a U.S. Bureau of Land Management base camp at which crews spent the summer months repairing damaged fences, washed-out roads, and doing other maintenance chores. By the first of October, they had gone for the winter, leaving a six-horse corral and open stable, plus several stacks of firewood.

As the hunt date approached, Mike and I talked at least once a week. His guide season would be over by then, and he had invited a couple of friends of his to join us to hunt deer, ducks, and sage grouse.

Shopping for the hunt, I visited our local farmer's market and found a wide variety of sweet peppers, green beans, golden and red delicious apples, and Bosc pears. When I added seven different species of basil, thyme, oregano, sage, and fennel from our home garden, plus some smoked king salmon and a large fillet of ling cod my father had given us, I knew we'd be eating well! Mike's friends, however, cancelled the day before I arrived in Missoula; so when Mike added a rack of lamb, T-bone steaks, several bottles of top-shelf liquor and very fine wine "leftover" from his guide service business, we were sure we wouldn't go hungry!

We transferred all of my food and gear to Mike's truck, finally leaving Missoula at 7:00 p.m.—with a five-hour drive ahead. Undaunted, we grabbed a couple of espressos and blasted eastward into the night, stopping for gas in Great Falls. We left the highway about thirty miles north of the Missouri River, taking a dirt and gravel track for the last seventy miles.

We finally arrived at the encampment after midnight. It was thirty degrees under amazingly bright, clear skies, and we quickly transferred our gear into the open stable, then set about erecting Mike's four-man tent. I've had a sensitive back since having fusion surgery in 1974, so I prepared for Montana's worst with three thick foam pads (which I offered to share with Mike) and two sub-zero sleeping bags. By the time everything was ready, my "royal" bed was nearly a foot high! Mike laughed as he curled up on a single memory foam pad with his chocolate lab, Belle.

Before I climbed into my bed, Mike asked if I'd ever seen the aurora borealis. I hadn't, so he told me to step out of the tent and look to the north. The horizon shimmered and glowed with the amazing phenomenon, minimizing, but not overshadowing, the immenseness and beauty of the crystal-clear night sky across which the Milky Way galaxy cut a wide swath. I stood in awe for several minutes before I remembered that it was freezing and all I was wearing was boxers and a T-shirt.

The next morning after breakfast, we headed out for the day. We soon spotted the bright-white rumps of several animals, but even Mike's 60-power spotting scope was all but useless when the animals were two and three miles away.

After several hours, Mike suggested that we hunt grouse along a narrow ridge covered with stubby juniper bushes and pine trees he had seen up the road ahead. Belle led the way as we walked quietly up the ridge. Stepping between knee-high shrubs, I saw feathers and other signs that grouse frequented the area. Almost as if on cue, three birds burst from the undergrowth just beyond the lip of the ridge several yards in front of Mike. He shot once but missed.

As the echo of his shot died, we saw a herd of thirteen antelope about three hundred yards down the hill. Mike didn't have to say a word: I raced back down to the truck to exchange my shotgun for my rifle. We spent over an hour watching the small band work their way down and across the hill, now nearly a half-mile below us.

As they stopped to feed, I dropped off the edge of the ridge into the bottom of a ravine that would take me on a parallel course to where they had bedded. I worked my way down the ravine, crawling to where I could see the bedded herd less than eighty yards away. I settled in to wait until they rose to feed, peering alternately through my 3 to 9×50 riflescope and my 8×30 binoculars. The buck in the group had decent horns that hooked inward in the shape of a heart, but after twenty minutes of studying him, I decided to pass.

Over the next two days, we drove miles of dirt roads and spotted several different herds of antelope but weren't satisfied with what we saw. One afternoon, though, as we rounded a lazy bend in the round, we saw the glint of sunshine off a stock pond a half-mile away. Mike's spotting scope quickly confirmed there were ten to twelve ducks, and that there was another pond a little further down the same gully to the left. With Belle in the lead again, we dropped into a ravine that led to the ponds.

We were soon in place on the down-slope side of the lower pond. Creeping, side by side, up to the rim, we rose to shoot, completely surprising the ducks. They exploded from the water, and we quickly dropped four of the five drakes in the flock.

The ducks on the second pond were on high alert following the commotion at the lower pond. As we popped up over the edge of the levee, we saw that they had swum to the far side of the water—almost, but not quite, out of gun range. When the shooting stopped, we were a little disappointed at having only two, but seven birds in less than an hour wasn't bad!

On the fourth morning, we spotted a herd of antelope in a wide-open plateau several miles ahead. Mike pulled the truck off the road, and we dropped down to a small creek that encircled the plateau. Finally reaching a point along the edge of the field that allowed a clear view, we determined that the animals were four hundred yards away, but completely unaware of our presence. I wasn't comfortable with such a long shot, but finally caved in to Mike's urging and attempted a shot at the large herd buck. A cloud of dust erupted when the bullet struck the ground at least ten yards short of my target and the herd bolted.

We had come nearly a half mile down the creek, but we covered the distance back in half the time in hopes of intercepting the herd as they left the plateau. We had noticed two fences crossing the field between the antelope and their escape route, and we hoped that those fences would slow them down enough to allow us to reach the intercept point before the herd.

As we reached the spot where the herd would pass, two does appeared in front of us, followed in single file by several others. I dropped to the ground, pushing my backpack in front of me for a rest. Finally the buck showed himself, then stopped to see what had bothered the does. I squeezed the trigger, and the buck immediately whirled and bolted straight away from us.

We found the monarch less than sixty yards from where he had stood when I pulled the trigger. Kneeling beside the buck, Mike placed a sprig of sagebrush in its mouth—a time-honored send-off practiced by woodsmen in Europe. He was truly magnificent, sporting fourteen-inch horns with pronounced "cutters." Later that day, as we crossed the Missouri River on a car barge and wound our way back to Missoula, Mike told me that my buck was the largest taken in that area for more than twenty years.

Chick Peas and Chicken Livers on Crostini

Ingredients:

- 4 cups chicken soup base or stock
- 1 cup dried chickpeas, soaked overnight in cold water
- 6 garlic cloves, leaving 4 whole and peeling and mincing the remaining two
- 3 bay leaves
- ½ lb. chicken livers, rinsed and trimmed of fat
- 4 tbsp. extra-virgin olive oil, divided
- kosher salt and medium grind white pepper, to taste
- 3 scallions, white and light green parts cut crosswise into thin slices (about 3 cups total)
- 1 tbsp. flat-leaf parsley, coarsely chopped
- 1 tbsp. white truffle oil
- 1 loaf of French bread or a baguette, cut crosswise into ¼-inch discs

Preparation:

1. Heat the chicken soup base or stock in a 2-quart soup pot over medium-high heat. Add the chickpeas, garlic, and bay leaves; and simmer for 45 to 50 minutes.
2. Remove the pot from the heat and let cool, then drain the chickpeas, reserving the liquid. Discard the bay leaves.
3. In a medium sauté pan, heat the butter over medium-high heat until melted. Add the chicken livers and the minced garlic and sauté, turning occasionally, until the mixture is browned all over and the livers are firm—but do not overcook. Remove the pan from the burner and let the livers cool, then transfer to a cutting board and chop coarsely.
4. Preheat the broiler to high.
5. Transfer the chickpeas to a large bowl and crush them with a potato masher. Add in 2 or 3 of the whole garlic cloves and stir, keeping the mixture coarse.
6. Add in the olive oil and the livers, and stir gently with a wooden spoon to mix. If the mixture is too thick, add some of the reserved stock.
7. Season to taste with salt and pepper, then stir in the scallions and parsley.
8. Place the bread slices on a cookie sheet and broil until lightly toasted—about 4 minutes.
9. Transfer the mixture to a serving bowl, drizzle with the truffle oil, and spoon over several toasts, reserving the remaining mixture and toasts for your guests to serve themselves.

Roasted Red Onion Salad with Garlic Vinaigrette

Vinaigrette Ingredients:

- 4 cloves garlic, peeled
- 1 large shallot, washed and peeled
- 2 tbsp. fresh parsley
- ¼ tsp. kosher salt
- ¼ tsp. coarsely ground black pepper
- 1 tbsp. white wine vinegar
- ½ cup olive oil

Preparation:

1. Place the garlic cloves and shallots in a food processor and pulse 2 or 3 times. Add the parsley, salt and pepper, and vinegar, then process for 10 seconds. Stop to scrape down the sides of the bowl and continue for another 10 seconds.
2. With the motor running, pour the oil through the food chute and process until thoroughly blended.

Salad Ingredients:

- 3 medium red onions, washed and cut crosswise into ¼-inch slices
- ¼ cup extra-virgin olive oil
- 4 cups mixed baby greens (red and green leaf lettuce, endive, watercress, etc.)
- ¼ cup toasted walnuts, coarsely chopped
- ¼ cup crumbled Bleu cheese

Preparation:

1. Preheat the oven to 500°F.
2. Place the onion slices on a lightly greased cookie sheet and drizzle with oil. Cook until the onion slices are slightly charred—about 10 minutes. Remove from the oven and let cool, then remove the outer skin from each piece. Set aside.
3. Reduce the oven temperature to 350°F and toast the walnuts on a cookie sheet for 10 minutes. Transfer to a cutting board and chop coarsely when cool enough to handle.
4. Place the greens in a large mixing bowl and add the walnuts and cheese, tossing gently to mix.
5. Transfer about a cup of the greens mixture to individual salad plates, top with several pieces of roasted onions, then drizzle with the vinaigrette.

Antelope Sausage and SunDried Tomato Risotto

Sausage Ingredients:

- 6 lb. antelope meat, cut into 1-inch cubes
- 4 lb. pork "Boston butt," cut into 1-inch cubes
- 1 small sweet onion, chopped finely
- 4 tbsp. minced garlic
- 2 tbsp. crushed dried thyme
- 2 tbsp. ground dried rosemary
- 2 tbsp. coarsely ground black pepper
- 2 tbsp. kosher salt
- 3 tsp. mustard seed
- 1 cup water
- 4 feet of 1½-inch diameter collagen casing

Preparation:

1. Cut the meats into 1-inch square cubes, then "par-freeze" the cubes by placing them in the freezer on a plate or in a plastic bag to chill until they are fairly firm to the touch, but not completely frozen. When the cubes are firm to the touch, remove them from the freezer and grind them in a heavy-duty food processor or a meat grinder with a medium blade into a large, nonreactive mixing bowl.

2. Add the spices, adding 1 cup of water as you stir, and mix thoroughly. Cover and refrigerate the mixture overnight.

3. Remove the mixture from the refrigerator and let it warm to room temperature.

4. Using a meat-stuffing machine, stuff the meat mixture into the collagen casing, making sure that the meat is packed tightly and all air pockets are squeezed out by stopping occasionally and working the casing with your hands. Tie off each casing when full and the air pockets have been eliminated. (You may need to pierce the casing with a sterile needle or pin to completely remove all of the air pockets.)

5. When all of the casings are filled and tied off, cook them in an oven or a smoker until the internal temperature reaches 150°F.

6. When they have cooled, the sausages that you don't need for the risotto can be double-wrapped in freezer paper or aluminum foil and ziplock freezer bags, and frozen for up to 1 year.

Risotto Ingredients:

- 2 beefsteak or heirloom tomatoes, halved crosswise and seeded
- 2 tbsp. olive oil
- ½ tbsp. dried thyme
- 2 coarsely chopped garlic cloves, plus 1 tsp. minced garlic
- kosher salt
- coarsely ground black pepper
- 6 cups chicken soup base or stock
- 4 slices of slab bacon, cut into ¼-inch dice
- 1 small yellow onion, minced
- ½ cup dry white wine
- 2 cups short- or medium-grain white rice
- 6 oz. sun-dried tomatoes, Julienned
- 1 lb. antelope sausage, sliced into ¼-inch rounds
- ¼ cup fat-free sour cream
- 1 cup grated parmesan cheese, plus ¼ cup for the table
- ½ cup fresh basil, chopped
- 3 tbsp. minced chives

Preparation:

1. Preheat the oven to 400°F.
2. Place the halved tomatoes, flat side down, in a small, lightly greased casserole dish. Sprinkle them sparingly with the olive oil, thyme, garlic, salt, and pepper.
3. Roast the tomatoes for 10 to 12 minutes, then remove them to cool for a few minutes. When cool enough to handle, remove the skins and place the tomatoes and any accumulated juices in a bowl.
4. Heat the chicken stock to a simmer, then keep it at a constant simmer.
5. In a large, heavy-bottomed stockpot, heat the remaining 1 tablespoon oil over medium heat. Add the bacon and cook for 4 minutes until lightly browned. Add the onion and cook, stirring constantly for 6 minutes. Add the minced garlic and cook for 2 minutes or until fragrant.
6. Add the rice and stir until it is coated with fat, then add the wine. Cook, stirring constantly, until the pan is nearly dry—about 3 minutes.
7. Add 1 cup of the stock to the rice. Cook, stirring, until the stock is absorbed— about 2 minutes.
8. Gradually add more stock, ¾ cup at a time, and stir gently until absorbed before adding more.
9. After 15 to 18 minutes, taste the rice for firmness and flavor, and add less stock at a time until the rice reaches the preferred texture.
10. Add the roasted tomatoes, sun-dried tomatoes, and sausage into the rice; and mix thoroughly. Then add the sour cream and 1 cup of the parmesan cheese. Taste, and add salt and pepper if needed.
11. Stir gently for another minute or so, then sprinkle in the basil and chives.
12. Spoon the risotto into large soup bowls and serve with the remaining parmesan cheese.

* Any lean venison is an acceptable alternative.

Bleu CheeseStuffed Pears

Ingredients:

- ¼ cup sugar
- 1 tbsp. all-purpose flour
- 1 tsp. cornstarch
- 1 large egg
- 1 egg yolk
- 1 cup non-fat Half-and-Half
- 2 tbsp. butter
- 1 tsp. vanilla extract
- 2 tbsp. non-fat cream cheese, softened
- 3 tbsp. crumbled Bleu cheese, softened
- 1 can pear halves, drained
- 2 tbsp. powdered sugar
- ¼ cup pecans, chopped

Preparation:

1. Combine the sugar, flour, and cornstarch in a small bowl, then set aside.
2. In a separate small bowl, beat the egg and egg yolk with a mixer until thick and pale, and add the sugar mixture, beating until thoroughly blended. Set aside.
3. In a small saucepan over medium-high heat, heat the Half-and-Half until hot (but do not boil). Stir about a fourth of the hot Half-and-Half into the egg mixture, then add the hot egg mixture to the remaining Half-and-Half.
4. Reduce the heat to low and cook, stirring constantly, until thickened. Remove from the heat and stir for another minute, then transfer to a medium mixing bowl and stir in the butter and vanilla. Cover and chill for at least 2 hours.
5. When ready to finish and serve, preheat the oven broiler to high.
6. In a small mixing bowl, combine the cream cheese and Bleu cheese, and beat until smooth, then fold into the chilled egg mixture.
7. Spoon the combined mixture into lightly greased ramekins and place a pear-half in each, cut side up. Sprinkle each pear-half with powdered sugar, then place the ramekins on a cookie sheet and broil, about 6 inches from the heat, for 1½ to 2 minutes or until lightly browned.
8. Sprinkle the walnuts over the top of each ramekin and broil for an additional 45 seconds. Remove and let cool slightly, then serve warm.

Sauted Spinach Ragout

Ingredients:

- coarse sea salt
- 1 tbsp. butter
- 6 cups (packed) baby spinach leaves
- 2 tbsp. sunflower oil
- 4 garlic cloves, peeled and minced
- 1½ tbsp. ginger, peeled and grated, divided
- 1 tsp. sesame oil
- 2 tbsp. pine nuts
- coarsely ground black pepper

Preparation:

1. Bring 3 quarts of lightly salted water to a boil in a 5-quart soup pot.
2. Add the spinach leaves and cook until wilted—about 20 seconds. Remove and drain.
3. Spread the leaves out on a mesh rack to cool quickly, then transfer it to a clean towel and squeeze out the remaining water. Set aside.
4. In a large sauté pan over medium heat, combine the oil, garlic, and ginger. Cook, stirring constantly, for 2 to 3 minutes.
5. Add the spinach leaves and cook, stirring, until heated through—about 1 minute—then stir in the sesame oil and the pine nuts. Add salt and pepper, if needed, to taste.
6. Transfer the mixture to a serving bowl and serve immediately.

Suggested Accompaniment

- *Merlot:* Hawkes Vineyard—Sonoma Valley, California, or Waterbrook—Walla Walla, Washington

Antelope Sausage and Sun-Dried Tomato Risotto

Savannah Stripers

A new job brought my family and me to Savannah in early 1999, and my folks wanted to visit as soon as they could. Dad wanted to do some fly fishing for red drum (also known as spot-tail bass and redfish), weakfish (also known as speckled trout), and striped bass. I asked around for a good guide and was referred to Captain Matt.

The day of our trip was beautiful—seventy-five degrees and clear, with only a gentle breeze wafting out of the east. We quickly loaded our gear into Capt. Matt's boat while he checked his supply of flies and provisions. Dad told Capt. Matt that he had done some online research and had tied up a bunch of flies. Capt. Matt's expression in response was skeptical but changed quickly when Dad showed him a dozen four-, five-, and six-inch streamers of various color patterns, plus several shrimp and crab imitators.

I hoped that that exchange would be a good omen as we pushed away from the dock and headed toward the Savannah River. Capt. Matt explained that the striped bass had started to move upstream as the water temperature had begun to drop. South Carolina and Georgia coastal rivers experience strong tidal action, and when the water temperature at the beaches soars to near ninety degrees, the river's water temperature is also high, so striped bass wait offshore in cooler ocean water before beginning their spawning run. It was early November, and the water temperature had finally dropped enough to bring them upriver.

Once in the Savannah River, Capt. Matt opened the throttles for a quick run upriver to the north side of Hutchinson Island. Passing under the concrete pilings of a railroad trestle, Capt. Matt pointed at a shallow, grassy area and said there'd be both reds and trout hunting along the edges in search of shrimp and mud minnows. Dad, being a much better caster than I, stood at the bow while I took position next to Capt. Matt at the stern, and we began to work our flies into small pockets and eddies around the weeds and grasses.

Dad quickly had a couple of light strikes, but between the current and the lack of commitment by the fish, he wasn't able to make a hook up. I also had a strike or two, but had trouble keeping my fly from snagging the grass blades. We gave it a valiant effort for a little over a half hour when Capt. Matt said that the tide was changing and that we needed to move to the trestles.

He positioned the boat about thirty yards upriver from the pilings and dropped anchor, then attached a basketball-sized float with a quick-release clip to the anchor line and a thirty-foot line from the float to the boat. This allowed him to use the engines as rudders to maneuver the boat to various positions along the arc created with the thirty-foot rope.

He quickly explained that stripers lay in wait at the base of the pilings for food fish to pass by above them, and as the outgoing tide picked up speed, the small fish weren't strong enough to swim against it and were swept through the trestles. We quickly selected a couple of streamer flies that would resemble the menhaden, then cast them from each side of the boat so they'd be swung by the current down and across the upriver side of the trestles.

On my third cast, a striper slashed the surface behind my fly, and I felt a slight tug on the line. I quickly raised the rod tip to sink the hook, but the fish was gone. Two casts later, Dad's fly was also hit. Surging from the depths, a fish attacked his fly and dove back toward dark water. Expertly planting the hook, Dad raised his rod tip and began to work the fish up and away from the pilings. "Don't let him get back into the trestle—they're covered with barnacles!" Capt. Matt shouted as he reached to unhitch the boat from the float.

As the boat began to float, stern-first, downriver, Capt. Matt expertly guided the boat between the pilings as the fish ran out ahead of us. Once through the trestle, we came broadside to allow Dad to play the fish; and ten minutes later, Capt. Matt boated the scrappy four-and-a-half-pound fish for a quick photo op.

Capt. Matt released the fish unharmed and headed back to the float. Within a couple of minutes, we were reattached to the float and had begun casting when we heard several loud splashes to our right and saw several stripers hitting a school of menhaden. Capt. Matt quickly repositioned, but within minutes, the turmoil had subsided. Figuring that they probably hadn't gone far, we cast our flies and watched as they swung toward the pilings. I began to strip line as my fly danced near one of the pilings, and on about the third pull, the water surface exploded as a large fish smacked my fly. This time, I was ready and reared back firmly but gently to set the hook.

As Dad had, I kept the fish away from the pilings; and we floated backward through the pilings into open water, where the fish circled the boat then dove for the safety of deep water. Although I hadn't battled stripers before either, it felt like a substantial fish, so I was careful to avoid "horsing" him too much.

Within a few minutes, I brought the tired fish alongside the boat, where Capt. Matt slipped a fish gripper onto the fish's jaw and lifted him into the boat. "Eleven nine" Capt. Matt said. "That's a very nice fish!"

We took a few photos, released the fish, and ran back through the pilings to our anchor spot. Wanting to get back to the marina before the remaining light ran out, Capt. Matt raised the anchor while Dad and I stowed our rods and gear, then we roared back to the Bull River Marina with great memories of our Savannah Stripers!

Parmesan, Onion, and Olive Tart

Ingredients:

- 2 tbsp. butter, softened to room temperature
- 2 tbsp. extra-virgin olive oil
- 2 cups finely chopped onion
- 1 clove garlic, minced
- ¼ tsp. salt
- ¼ tsp. coarsely ground black pepper
- 1 tsp. fresh thyme leaves, divided
- 2 tbsp. flour
- ½ cup Kalamata olives, pitted and minced
- ¾ cup Parmesan cheese, grated
- 3 eggs, divided
- one 8- or 9-inch pie crust

Preparation:

1. Heat the butter and oil in a large sauté pan over medium heat. Add the onion and cook, stirring, until translucent—5 to 7 minutes.
2. Remove the pan from the heat and add the garlic, salt, pepper, 1/2 teaspoon of the thyme leaves, flour, olives, and cheese, stirring to combine thoroughly.
3. In a medium mixing bowl, beat 2 of the eggs, and add a small amount of the onion mixture; stir quickly to temper eggs. Add the remaining onion mixture and stir to combine, then set aside to cool.
4. Preheat the oven to 350°F.
5. Add the cooled filling to the piecrust. Beat the remaining egg in a small dish and brush it onto the edges of the piecrust. Place the pie tin on a foil-lined baking sheet and bake for 35 to 40 minutes, or until the top is set.
6. Remove from the oven and sprinkle with the remaining ½ teaspoon of fresh thyme.
7. Let cool a little, then cut into wedges, and serve immediately.

Hearts of Palm Salad

Ingredients:

- 3 tbsp. extra-virgin olive oil
- 2 tbsp. tarragon vinegar
- ¼ tsp. Dijon mustard
- ¼ tsp. kosher salt
- ¼ tsp. coarsely ground black pepper
- 2 cups (one 14-oz. can) hearts of palm, drained and sliced
- 1/3 cup red bell pepper, diced
- ½ cup artichoke heart, drained and sliced
- 1/3 cup Kalamata olives, pitted and halved lengthwise
- 3 cups packaged mixed salad greens (baby spinach, endive, baby romaine, etc.)
- 2 hardboiled eggs, cut crosswise into thin slices
- 1 cup cherry tomatoes, halved

Preparation:

1. Combine the dressing ingredients in an airtight container and shake vigorously to mix. Chill until the salad is ready to serve.
2. Combine the hearts of palm, peppers, artichoke hearts, and olives in a large serving bowl.
3. Pour the dressing over the palm, peppers, artichoke hearts, and olives; and toss gently. Cover and refrigerate for at least 1 hour.
4. When ready to serve, place the mixed greens on chilled individual salad plates, divide the heart of palm mixture evenly over the plates, and arrange the tomatoes and hardboiled egg slices over the top.

Macadamia NutEncrusted Striped Bass

Ingredients:

- 4 oz. (about 1 cup) coarsely chopped macadamia nuts
- 1/2 cup plain bread crumbs
- 2 tbsp. all-purpose flour
- ½ tsp. medium-fine grind white pepper
- ½ tsp. kosher salt
- 1/4 cup butter, melted
- 2 tbsp. extra-virgin olive oil
- 2 cloves minced garlic
- 2 striped bass fillets, about 4 oz. each

Preparation:

1. Mix the nuts, crumbs, flour, pepper, and salt together in a small bowl, then slowly pour in the melted butter, stirring constantly to ensure thorough mixing.
2. In a 9-inch heavy-bottomed, oven-safe sauté pan, heat the oil over medium heat until shimmering
3. Add the garlic and sauté until it starts to turn golden brown (about 3 or 4 minutes)
4. While the garlic cooks, (i) pre-heat the broiler, and (ii) rinse the fillets and pat them dry with a paper towel.
5. Place the fillets, skin side down, on a cutting board or a clean countertop, then spread the macadamia nut mixture onto each fillet, pressing it gently into the flesh. Once each fillet is coated, place them into the sauté pan, skin side down. Cook until the flesh begins to firm up— about 12–15 minutes.
6. Remove the pan from the burner and transfer to the oven/broiler. Broil for 5 to 6 minutes, or until the coating begins to brown.
7. Remove the pan from the oven/broiler to a cool burner on the stovetop, then gently lift each fillet onto a serving platter with one or two spatulas.

* Grouper and snapper are acceptable alternatives.

Candied Acorn Squash

Ingredients:

- 4 acorn squash
- 1/3 cup butter, melted
- 1/3 cup brown sugar, packed
- 1/3 cup maple syrup
- ½ tsp. ground cinnamon

Preparation:

1. Preheat oven to 375°F.
2. Cut each squash in half lengthwise, then scoop out and discard the seeds. Cut each half crosswise into 1-inch slices.
3. Arrange the slices slightly overlapping, in a lightly greased 13×9×2-inch baking dish.
4. Bake, covered, for 35 minutes.
5. Combine melted butter, brown sugar, syrup, and cinnamon; and spoon mixture over the squash slices.

Suggested Accompaniment

- *Chenin Blanc:* Dry Creek Vineyard—Sonoma Valley, California, or Graham Beck Game Reserve—South Africa
- *Chardonnay:* 14 Hands—Columbia Valley, Washington

Macadamia Nut-Encrusted Striped Bass

The 10 11 Bucks

We all remember the tragedy of September 11, 2001, and how it has affected many aspects of our lives from that day forward. Especially with respect to travel, the ease with which we used to be able to move through airports and train stations with firearms seems to have been changed forever.

Those were my thoughts in the weeks following the terrorist attack as I planned a Montana elk-and-mule deer hunt with my good friend Mike, owner of High Plains Drifter in Missoula. I was concerned about traveling with my .30–06 rifle from Savannah, Georgia, to Missoula, Montana, because nearly every day, there were reports about new security measures at airports around the country.

As my hunt approached, I spoke with several people at the airport and was told that I should have no problem checking my gun through to Missoula, but that I would need to get to the airport two hours prior to the scheduled 8:05 a.m. departure time with my gun and ammunition in a locked carrying case and clear identification tags.

My flight was on a Wednesday morning, so there would be fewer travelers than earlier in the week. I arrived at the check-in counter at 5:50 a.m. to find few people in the airport, much less checking in for a flight two hours from then. After I confirmed my tickets and identification, the attendant politely asked me to open the gun case, confirmed everything to be in order, and handed me my boarding pass and baggage receipts.

The good news was that I had checked in, cleared security, and was sitting at the departure gate in less than five minutes. The bad news was that the Starbucks kiosk didn't open for another half hour, and I had two hours to kill before departure!

Arriving in Missoula exactly on time, I quickly found Mike in the baggage pick-up area. My bag and gun case had already been delivered to the "special" baggage window, and when I presented my baggage ticket to the clerk at the counter and commented that the new security measures didn't seem to be causing any problems, he said, "This is Montana, sir. We'd have a real problem if people couldn't bring their guns to hunt here!"

An hour later, Mike and I were on our way out of Missoula under clear skies, headed southeast toward the town of Dillon. After a four-hour drive, we pulled into a small, secluded glen off the side of a logging road, and I quickly felt the effects of the long day of travel and the 7,500-foot altitude as we began unloading and setting up camp.

We hunted hard for elk for two days without seeing anything. That night, Mike suggested that we hunt another area a few miles south of camp for mule deer. So on the third morning—again well before dawn—we drove to the west side of a deep canyon just north of Dillon, planning to hunt the ridges west of the canyon. We reached our destination almost two hours later, looking down on the highway and the river from a vista nearly a thousand feet above the canyon floor. "This is spectacular!" I said, admiring the view.

"It'll be even more spectacular if we can catch up with those deer!" Mike replied, pointing up a draw to his left at a band of deer making their way across a shale slide. We split up to cover more of the wide-open territory, and twenty minutes later, I saw more deer making their way down and across the other side of the ridge on which I was walking. I made sure not to "skyline" myself to the deer as they made their way to the bottom of the draw and bedded down. I crawled up next to a clump of sagebrush and quickly spotted three bucks—two two-by-two's (or "fork-horns") and a three-by-four. Sliding my fanny pack in front of me to create a good rest, I eased my rifle into position; but after studying the bucks for fifteen minutes, I decided I could do better and eased my way back down the other side of the crest.

It was late afternoon when we met at the truck for the drive back to camp. Driving slowly, we were discussing which areas we should hunt the next day when, suddenly, two big bucks burst from cover just below the roadbed to our left. Mike slammed on the brakes and I piled out of the truck, shoving bullets into my gun and trying to keep an eye on the deer as they bounced across the hillside in front of us. As they slowed to look back at us, I dropped to my belly for a steady shot.

Boom! Nothing happened for several seconds, then both deer bolted again, one crossing the road in front of us. I leapt to my feet and took off after him.

As I clambered over some large rocks at the side of the road, I slipped and slammed to the ground, knocking the glasses off my face and bending them in the process. I managed to keep my rifle off the ground but lost a shot opportunity as I struggled to get the glasses back on my head. As I struggled, the buck crossed back over the road and quickly caught up with its partner, and they both bounded straight down the steep hillside to the bottom of the ravine nearly five hundred yards below.

By this time, Mike had caught up with me and asked what had happened. I explained everything as I straightened the unnatural kink in one of the temples of my glasses. Laughing together, we grabbed our jackets and packs, and tore off down the hill, keeping an eye on the bucks as we went. As we came to a flat, level area about twenty yards wide, Mike whispered, "They're both at the bottom of the ravine right below us." Peering through his binoculars, he continued, "The one on the right is better, but both of them are nice."

"How far?" I asked as I crawled to his side. "Three hundred yards," he answered.

I fired, seeing a small cloud of dust erupt from the bank in front of the buck. Knowing that I'd aimed too high, I lowered the riflescope's cross hairs from about two inches above the buck's shoulder to the base of its neck. *Boom!*

"You got him!" Mike exclaimed quietly. As I recovered from the recoil, I saw that the buck had dropped to its chest. Within seconds, however, it rose to its feet and tried to follow its partner. I chambered another round and leveled the scope on the wounded deer, but before I could pull the trigger, he fell sideways into a cluster of sagebrush bushes.

Mike headed back up to the truck to get his two-wheeled game cart while I made my way down to the bottom of the ravine. By the time Mike returned, it was pitch dark and getting cold. "That's a big deer!" he said as he looked it over. "I'd guess him to be around two-fifty, and he's got a nice rack too!"

We knew that the temperature would be cool enough that night that spoilage wouldn't be an issue, but I was concerned about coyotes. Mike assured me that they wouldn't come near the deer if we hung a few pieces of our clothing on the surrounding bushes, so we finished cleaning the animal and hung some of our socks on the brush around him.

The next morning, before we retrieved my buck, Mike drove up the ridge to see if the second buck had remained in the area. We left the truck at the end of the road and had gone barely a hundred yards when Mike saw it feeding further down the hill near some pines.

Seconds later, Mike's gun roared, dropping the buck instantly. Once he confirmed that it was dead, I ran to get the truck as Mike field dressed his buck, and we soon had it loaded onto the flatbed trailer.

As we filled in our tags, I noticed that it had been exactly thirty days since the twin-tower attacks, so I said to Mike, "I guess we got ourselves a couple of 10/11 bucks!"

Chunky Elk Venison Chili

Rub Ingredients:

- 2 lb. elk shoulder or rump roast, trimmed of fat and tissue, and cut into ½-inch cubes
- 1 tbsp. granulated garlic
- 2 tbsp. powdered chipotle chili
- 1 tbsp. ground cumin
- ½ tsp. dried oregano
- ¼ tsp. ground cinnamon
- ⅛ tsp. cayenne pepper
- ¼ tsp. ground cloves
- 1 tbsp. kosher salt
- 1 tbsp. coarsely ground black pepper

Chili Ingredients:

- 2 lb. marinated elk shoulder or rump roast
- 2 tbsp. extra-virgin olive oil, divided
- 2 onions—1 yellow and 1 red—finely chopped
- 4 garlic cloves, minced
- ¼ cup smoked paprika
- 3 tbsp. chili powder
- 1 tbsp. ground cumin
- ½ tsp. dried oregano
- ¼ tsp. ground cinnamon
- ⅛ tsp. cayenne pepper
- ¼ tsp. ground cloves
- ¾ tsp. kosher salt
- 1 tsp. coarsely ground black pepper
- 1 can (28 oz.) diced tomatoes
- 1 can (15 oz.) red kidney beans— rinsed and drained
- 1 can (15 oz.) great northern or navy beans— rinsed and drained
- ¼ cup apple cider vinegar
- 2 bay leaves
- 1 cup shredded cheddar cheese (optional)

Rub Preparation:

1. Place the cubed meat into a nonreactive bowl or container
2. Mix the remaining ingredients together thoroughly, then rub the meat, ensuring that each cube is entirely covered, then seal the bowl with plastic wrap and refrigerate overnight.
3. Remove the meat from the refrigerator when ready for cooking.

Chili Preparation:

1. Preheat 1 tbsp. of the oil in a 5–6-quart Dutch oven over medium-high heat.
2. Add half of the meat and cook until browned all over. Transfer to a plate, add the other tablespoon of oil, and repeat with the other half of the meat.
3. Add the onions to the drippings and cook, stirring gently, for about 5 minutes or until the onions begin to soften. Add the garlic and cook for another minute, then add the remaining dry ingredients and cook, stirring, for 5 minutes.
4. Add the tomatoes and liquid, beans, vinegar, bay leaves, and the meat (including juices that may have accumulated on the plate).
5. Reduce to medium-low, then cover and simmer for at least 2 hours, stirring occasionally. Taste from time to time and add seasonings as needed.
6. Remove bay leaves and serve.

Broiled Romaine with Toasted Pecans, Parmesan, and Anchovy Dressing

Ingredients:

- 4 anchovy fillets (or 1 tbsp. anchovy paste)
- 2 tsp. minced garlic
- ½ tsp. kosher salt
- ½ cup extra-virgin olive oil
- 3 tsp. lemon juice
- 2 hearts of romaine lettuce
- 2/3 cup toasted pecans, chopped
- 1 cup Asiago or Parmesan cheese, shaved

Preparation:

1. Puree the anchovy fillets, garlic, and salt in a small food processor. Add the olive oil in a slow stream, pureeing into a creamy sauce. Stir in the lemon juice; taste and add more lemon juice and/or salt if needed. Set aside.
2. Split the romaine hearts in half, lengthwise, and brush with the anchovy sauce.
3. Place the lettuce halves on a hot barbeque grate or in a 12-inch heavy-bottomed sauté pan heated over medium-high heat until they sizzle—about 2 to 3 minutes—then flip and repeat.
4. Transfer the lettuce halves to individual serving plates with the cut sides up, garnish with pecan pieces, and drizzle on some more dressing.
5. Shave the Parmesan cheese over the top of each lettuce half and serve immediately.

Suggested Accompaniment

- *Cabernet Sauvignon:* Baron V—Columbia Valley, Washington, or Greg Norman—Limestone Coast, Australia

Chunky Venison Chili

Bahamas Bones

In early 2003, my dad won a silent auction at a Trout Unlimited banquet in Seattle and invited me to join him on Long Island in the Bahamas to pursue bonefish. He said I could invite someone from our "new" life in Savannah, and Kevin—a friend, neighbor, and work colleague—jumped at the chance.

Kevin and I met Dad in Nassau before the flight to Long Island, and enjoyed a scenic flight over the azure waters that connected the islands of the Bahamas.

The lodge at which we stayed was a comfortable house perched on a ridge dissecting the island, and our view out over the Atlantic to the east was spectacular. A short walk down a dirt road to the shoreline gave us an opportunity to see some beautiful rock formations and try to catch a fish in a large, crystal-clear cove sheltered from the roaring surf.

The next morning, we met our guides Freddy and Juan over breakfast. Freddy explained that we would fish all week along a peninsula to the south and west of the lodge that extended almost three miles into the azure waters of the Atlantic. The north side used to be a sea salt "plantation" where a dozen or so large flats, each a quarter mile square, had been bulldozed out of a former marshland. Canals had then been gouged along the edges of the flats to allow the tide to fill the flats with seawater and provide access for the salt harvesting equipment. When the tide receded, salt would dry on the flats and the harvesters would vacuum it up before the incoming tide flooded the flats again.

There was also a deep channel that wended its way from the ocean to an inland bay where the islanders kept their boats. Each morning, we would motor out the channel and take one of the canals to a salt flat or continue out toward the ocean.

Paul took Dad and I to a salt flat, and we were stalking our first school of bonefish an hour later. Walking about twenty yards apart and wading slowly, we had to be careful not to splash the foot-deep water as we waded toward a feeding school, watching the tails of some of the large fish break the surface as they rooted in the sand for prey.

Dad made a beautiful cast, dropping his shrimp imitator ten feet in front of the lead fish. He let it sink for a second, then quickly stripped in the line with a rhythmic motion. On the second cast, a large bonefish hammered the fly and took off for the ocean, peeling line from the reel. Dad started to raise the rod tip to create some resistance, but Freddy told him to keep it pointed right at the fish for the first couple of runs.

Within a few seconds, the feisty fish was nearly fifty yards out. With Freddy providing expert advice, though, Dad soon had it turned and headed back our way, allowing him to take back most of the line the fish had torn from the reel. After three strong runs, the fish finally allowed Freddy to land, unhook, and release it.

We fished the flat for another three hours, each catching and releasing several fish, before it was time for lunch. The tide had receded, leaving the flat almost completely high and dry, so we sat on the levee overlooking the canal. A large, dark shadow, which Freddy identified as a barracuda, drifted across a sandy patch. He explained that they usually ambushed bonefish in deep pockets in the canal at low tide but would also come out onto the flats to hunt.

We fished several pools in the canal until the incoming tide filled the flats again, and, after a long but enjoyable day, decided to head in. Paul and Kevin were already at the lodge when Freddy, Dad, and I arrived. We exchanged stories about our days as we sipped a nice single-malt scotch, and Kevin showed us a picture of a twenty-two-inch bonefish he had foul hooked, causing Paul to keep it.

The next morning, Kevin and I paired up with Paul and headed for the ocean flats, which took us nearly an hour to reach. On the boat ride out, Paul explained that bonefish schools on the ocean flats can have several thousand fish in them, and that they fed by digging up the sand with their noses, creating clouds of silt called "muds." Once he figured out what direction the school was feeding, he would position us ahead of the mud, and we would cast into it.

Soon after we got into position, Paul spotted a large "mud" and steered us toward it. As we approached the feeding fish, Kevin and I cast toward the milky cloud and, within seconds, we each hooked a fish. Fortunately, they took off in opposite directions, so we didn't have to worry about our lines becoming tangled.

"Keep your eyes on them," Paul said as they raced away from the boat. "Black-tipped reef sharks feed on bonefish when they mud like this, and there's a good chance a shark will come after them!"

No sooner had he said it than my line went slack, and I figured that a shark had gotten my fish. As I started to reel in my line, it tightened and began to pull away from us.

"You've got a shark!" Paul said as he watched my line. "Hopefully he'll break off quickly."

As Kevin brought his fish to the side of the boat for Paul to unhook and release, the six-foot black-tipped reef shark on my line raced toward the boat. Fifteen feet from the bow, it burst out of the water, spiraling straight at me! Fortunately, its arc took it back into the water before it hit me or the boat, but the sight of that shark hurtling directly at me was both mesmerizing and terrifying!

On the third day, I went out "solo" with Paul. About halfway across the flat, Paul pointed at a dark shape fifty yards in front of us. He told me to switch to a heavier rod and rig it with a wire leader and a six-inch streamer. He asked me if I'd ever played a barracuda on a fly rod. I hadn't, so he explained that a big 'cuda would usually tail walk just like a tarpon and that I should point my rod tip at him when he jumped and lay the rod sideways when he ran.

Paul let the boat drift toward the large fish as I laid a cast to its left. When the fly hit the surface, I stripped it quickly back toward the boat. The huge fish swam after the fly, following it toward the boat with malicious intent. Then, as I swung the tip of the rod across the bow of the boat, the fish charged the fly, grabbing it and tearing away from us. I raised the rod tip enough to set the hook, then pointed it at the fish as it streaked away. Seconds later, it burst out of the water and "danced" over the surface, churning the shallow water with its tail.

As the large fish neared the boat, he took off again and the wire leader broke—the victim of a kink caused by one of the fish's violent headshakes. We followed the large fish, which Paul estimated to be at least thirty-five pounds, to a deep pool at the bottom end of the flat where it hovered—sulking—with the bright streamer fly still hooked at the side of its jaw.

That afternoon, we made our way back to the channel, deciding to troll a lure for jack crevalle. As we reached a large pool, we saw a school of fish patrolling the far edge of the deep pool of crystal-clear water. Seconds later, the reel sang as a good-sized jack grabbed the fly and headed toward the depths. The fish was strong but it tired quickly, and Paul was soon able to land it and drop it into his small ice chest.

The next day was our last day on the water. Dad wanted to continue to fish the salt flats while Kevin and I wanted to head back out to the ocean. On the way in after a long day on the water, Paul told us that he and his friends caught conchs nearby, and we quickly decided to catch a couple ourselves. The water was shallow enough for us to see greenish-brown "bumps" on the sandy bottom that Paul told us were conchs, and we quickly gathered a dozen. Paul was surprised—but not happy—that we wanted some of the shells intact. Getting them out without breaking the shell was apparently a lot of work, but Paul finally agreed to clean three shells apiece for us and handle the rest "his" way so that he could make conch fritters that night.

Paul presented the shells to us the next morning before we headed out—a beautiful keepsake of our Bahamas Bones adventures!

Bahamian Conch Fritters

Fritter Ingredients:

- 1 qt. vegetable oil
- ¾ cup all-purpose flour
- 1 large egg
- ½ cup milk
- ¼ tsp. cayenne pepper
- kosher salt, to taste
- coarsely ground black pepper, to taste
- 1 cup conch meat, cleaned, rinsed, and coarsely chopped
- ½ sweet onion, peeled and coarsely chopped
- ½ green bell pepper, finely chopped
- ½ yellow bell pepper, finely chopped
- ½ red bell pepper, finely chopped
- 2 celery stalks, finely chopped
- 2 large garlic cloves, peeled and finely chopped

Dipping Sauce Ingredients:

- 2 tbsp. ketchup
- 2 tbsp. fresh lime juice
- 1 tbsp. reduced-fat mayonnaise
- ½ tsp. Tabasco sauce
- kosher salt and coarsely ground black pepper, to taste

Preparation:

1. Heat the oil in large pot or deep fryer to 365°F (185°C).
2. In a bowl, mix the flour, egg, and milk.
3. Season with cayenne pepper, seasoning salt, salt, pepper, and red pepper flakes.
4. Mix in the conch meat; red, yellow, and green peppers; onion; celery; and garlic.
5. Drop the batter by rounded tablespoons into the hot oil and fry until golden brown.
6. Remove the basket or with slotted spoon and drain on paper towels.
7. Season, to taste (again), with salt and pepper.

Preparation:

1. Mix the ketchup, lime juice, mayonnaise, hot sauce, salt, and pepper together in a small mixing bowl.
2. Serve dipping sauce on the side with the fritters.

Collard Greens with Smoked Ham

Ingredients:

- ¼ cup extra-virgin olive oil
- 1 tbsp. butter
- 2 tbsp. garlic, diced
- 3 cups chicken soup base or stock
- 1 cup smoked ham, shredded or coarsely chopped
- 2 bunches collard greens; rinsed, trimmed, and chopped
- kosher salt and coarsely ground black pepper, to taste
- ¼ cup champagne vinegar
- ½ tsp. crushed red pepper flakes (optional)

Preparation:

1. Heat olive oil in a large stockpot over medium heat.
2. Add the garlic and sauté until it is light brown, then pour in the chicken soup base, and add the ham.
3. Reduce the heat to medium low, cover the pot, and simmer for 30 minutes.
4. Add the collard greens and turn the heat up to medium high. Let the greens cook for about 45 minutes, stirring occasionally.
5. Reduce the heat to medium, and season with salt and pepper to taste.
6. Continue to cook the greens until they are tender— about 55 to 60 minutes.
7. Drain the greens, reserving the liquid, and transfer them to a large serving bowl. Stir in the vinegar and red pepper flakes if desired.
8. Use the reserved liquid to reheat leftovers.

BlackTipped Reef Shark ShishKebabs
with Pineapple and Rosemary

Ingredients:

- 3 cups buttermilk
- 2 lb. shark fillets cut into 1½-inch cubes
- 4 tbsp. butter
- 2 large shallots, minced
- 1 tbsp. orange zest; grated
- ¼ cup orange juice
- 1 each green, red, and orange bell pepper, cored and cut into 1½-inch pieces
- 1 large sweet onion, peeled and cut into 1½-inch pieces
- 12 to 16 large pineapple chunks
- ¼ cup peanut oil
- 3 tbsp. rosemary, divided

Preparation:

1. In a wide, shallow, nonreactive dish or bowl, place the shark cubes in the buttermilk and refrigerate for at least an hour before cooking.
2. Melt the butter in a small sauté pan over medium heat and cook the shallots until tender, stirring occasionally.
3. Whisk in the orange zest and juice, bring the mixture to a boil, stir, and remove from the heat.
4. Prepare a charcoal fire in the barbeque.
5. Remove the shark cubes from the buttermilk, then rinse and pat them dry with paper towels.
6. Thread the shark cubes, peppers, onion, and orange sections alternating, onto four 10-inch metal skewers with fish, zucchini, onions, and orange quarters. Brush each skewer with peanut oil, then sprinkle 1 tablespoon of the rosemary over each skewer.
7. When the coals have a thin coat of white ash, spread them out evenly with a metal prod and place the cooking grates over the hot coals.
8. Sprinkle the remaining rosemary over the hot coals and grill the kabobs, rotating every 3 minutes, until the shark cubes begin to flake when tested with a fork.
9. Reheat the orange sauce, then transfer it to a serving bowl.
10. Serve the kabobs on individual platters and with the warmed orange sauce.

* Mako, or other shark species available at your fish market, is an acceptable option.

Tomato Salad with Mozzarella and Basil

Ingredients:

- 2 large beefsteak tomatoes, cut into 12 slices
- kosher salt and coarsely ground black pepper, to taste
- ½ lb. fresh mozzarella cheese, thinly cut into 24 slices
- ½ cup (packed) fresh basil leaves, washed and drained
- 2 tbsp. raspberry balsamic vinegar

Preparation:

1. Place a tomato slice on each of four individual salad plates. Sprinkle each of the tomato slices with a touch of salt and pepper, place two slices of the cheese and two basil leaves on top of each tomato slice, and repeat with two more layers.
2. Chill for at least 15 minutes, then serve immediately.

Suggested Accompaniment

- *Chardonnay:* 14 Hands—Columbia Valley, Washington

Black-Tipped Reef Shark Shish-Kebabs with Pineapple and Rosemary

Three Little Pigs

After moving my family from Seattle, Washington, to Savannah, Georgia, in 1999, one high priority was to learn about hunting and fishing in the area, and then to meet people who hunted and fished. I managed to meet a couple of guys at work who were willing to talk to me about Coastal Georgia's hunting and fishing opportunities.

The most fascinating game animal hunted by virtually every rednecked—oops, I meant red-blooded—son of a gun was wild hog, and Georgia is being overrun by them. They tear up farmland and eat crops before they can be harvested. On the other hand, the hogs are delicious, and they can be found on both private and public land.

In early March 2000, Tim, a colleague at work, invited me to join him and his friend, Danny, on a "cull" hunt in the Savannah National Wildlife Refuge. The morning of the hunt, my son, Luke, and I met Tim and his son and Danny at a boat launch on Abercorn Creek—a tributary of the Savannah River. We quickly had our gear loaded and Tim's and Danny's small boats in the water. The sky was clear as the sun rose, and we were all looking forward to the hunt.

Forty-five minutes later, running downstream and around several bends as we worked our way back into the refuge's remote creeks and islands, we found ourselves in an area of slow-moving, tan-colored water with overhanging limbs and deadfalls crossing the waterway. I wouldn't have been surprised if a banjo had started playing the theme from *Deliverance*!

Once Danny found his spot, we tied both boats to large trees, leaving extra line for when the tide receded. We all quickly loaded our guns and followed Danny through a thicket of bamboo, finding ourselves in a wet, swampy glade that seemed to go on in every direction for a several hundred yards.

"Spread out and we'll walk slowly north until the creek bends to the east," Danny instructed. He had no idea how glad I was that he knew where we were and where we were going, until he added, "Oh, and keep an eye out for snakes."

"What kind of snakes?" I asked anxiously.

"Copperheads and Cottonmouths," he replied as if it was a silly question.

About two hours later, we reached the end of the island and headed back to the boats. The tide had receded, leaving about five feet of exposed mucky goo. Fortunately, Danny had parked us next to a fallen log that we were able to use as a ramp to the boats.

A few minutes later, with Danny and Luke in the lead and out of sight beyond the next bend, we heard Danny's engine cut out. Tim figured that Danny had seen something because we hadn't gone more than two hundred yards. As we rounded the bend, we saw Danny leaning over the transom with his arm in the water up past his elbow.

A few second later, the head of a small hog popped out of the water as it swam for the bank. Danny quickly gunned his motor and headed for the same bank about ten yards further upstream. As the boat slid onto the slimy mud, Danny grabbed his 20-gauge shotgun and climbed over Luke's seat and onto the bank. The hog had climbed as far as it could in the foot-plus-deep mud and was looking for an escape route.

With Luke still pretty much paralyzed by the rapid sequence of events, Danny put one foot onto a large tree root and fired.

Boom!—quickly followed by "Shoot!" (Not his actual word.) If we had time to think about it, Tim and I would have both laughed out loud: Danny had tried for a head shot and had shot under the animal. He quickly extracted the used shell and plopped in another. The hog hadn't moved, so this time, Danny took a more careful aim before squeezing the trigger. *Boom!*

The pig let out a squeal that was louder than I imagined possible, but it didn't move. Danny climbed back into the boat, pushing it out of the muck and allowing it to drift down the creek a few yards until the bow was even with the hog. Gunning the motor again, he drove the boat up into the muck, a foot away from the hog. Again climbing quickly to the front of the boat, he reached over the shallow side and grabbed the critter by a front leg and its tail, hauled it into the boat, and dropped it onto the floorboard. Luke looked down in a mixture of terror and horror as the animal thrashed at his feet! Danny pushed the boat back out into the water and floated down to where Tim and his son and I had watched the whole crazy drama.

"I guess this makes you and Luke honorary rednecks, don't it?" Tim said as he gave Danny a high five.

Two years later, Danny and I headed to an area that Danny knew hadn't been hunted for several years. We cruised downriver for a mile until we came to a small "finger" off the main waterway and headed into the marsh. Finding a likely spot, I tied us to a limb that reached out over the water—again leaving plenty of extra line to allow for the receding tide—and we climbed up the bank onto a wide, flat area with widely spaced oak and gum trees and ankle-deep spring grasses.

We crept along about forty yards apart, our senses alert for any sign of movement, the sound of rustling brush or a telltale snort. We hadn't gone more than a hundred yards when I saw the shoulders of a small black pig above the top of the grass.

I whistled in Danny's direction to get his attention and signaled that I had seen a hog. Just then, another larger animal emerged from a small bush. I quickly changed my signal to "two," and Danny nodded his understanding. We both dropped to our bellies and took aim at the unsuspecting animals. When it was clear that we both had our targets lined up, Danny gave me the OK sign, and we both pulled the trigger. My target dropped instantly, just as Danny's gun roared. "Got 'em!" he shouted as he rose from a kneeling position.

We quickly took care of our field dressing chores, then wrapped each animal in a single cotton-mesh game bag and hung them from a low-hanging tree limb.

We hunted for a while longer before calling it quits for the day, then carefully made our way back to our hogs and shouldered them for the short walk back to the boat, happy with our quick but successful hunt.

French Onion and Shiitake Mushroom Soup

Ingredients:

- 2 tbsp. butter
- 4 medium sweet or red onions, halved laterally then thinly sliced vertically
- kosher salt and coarsely ground black pepper, to taste
- ½ cup Marsala wine
- 6 cups beef soup base or stock
- 2 cups water
- ¼ lb. (about 2 cups) sliced shiitake mushrooms with stems removed
- and discarded
- 1 loaf of French bread (or a baguette), sliced into ¼-inch discs
- 2 tsp. minced garlic
- 1 tbsp. Extra-virgin olive oil
- 1 cup shredded smoked cheddar cheese

Preparation:

1. Melt the butter over medium heat in a 4-quart soup pot. Add the onion and a little salt and pepper. Reduce the heat to medium low and cook, stirring occasionally to prevent charring, for 35 to 40 minutes, until the onions turn light brown. As long as they don't char, the longer the onions cook, the sweeter they will become.
2. Add the wine, stock, water, and mushrooms to the pot and stir, scraping the bottom of the pan to loosen any pieces stuck to the bottom of the pan. Bring the mixture to a boil, then lower to a simmer and cook for 35 minutes.
3. Preheat the broiler.
4. Place the bread discs on a foil-lined broiler pan and toast them under the broiler.
5. While the bread is toasting, mix the garlic and olive oil together, and spread a spoonful on each toast disc when it comes out of the oven.
6. Place four ovenproof soup bowls on a cookie sheet and ladle soup into each bowl, place two toast discs on top of the soup, and sprinkle on a small handful of the grated cheese. Slide the cookie sheet under the broiler and cook until the cheese melts—about 2 to 3 minutes— then serve immediately.

Roast Leg of Wild Boar

Marinade Ingredients:

- ¼ cup extra-virgin olive oil, plus 2 tbsp. for cooking
- ¼ cup minced Kalamata olives, pits removed
- 4 minced garlic cloves
- 1 tbsp. ground juniper berries
- 1 tbsp. anchovy paste
- ½ tsp. dried, ground rosemary
- ½ tsp. dried thyme
- ½ tsp. kosher salt
- ½ tsp. coarsely ground black pepper

Meat Rub Ingredients:

- ¼ cup extra-virgin olive oil, plus 2 tbsp. for cooking
- ¼ cup minced Kalamata olives, pits removed
- 4 minced garlic cloves
- 1 tbsp. ground juniper berries
- 1 tbsp. anchovy paste
- ½ tsp. dried, ground rosemary
- ½ tsp. dried thyme
- ½ tsp. kosher salt
- ½ tsp. coarsely ground black pepper

Preparation:

1. In a 1-gallon freezer bag, mix the oil, wine, vinegar, salt, and pepper. Place the meat in the bag, working it with your hands to coat all surfaces evenly. Refrigerate for 6 to 8 hours.

Preparation:

1. Mix all ingredients in food processor and pulse until thoroughly mixed.
2. Pre-heat the oven to 375°F.
3. Remove the roast from the refrigerator and rinse it under cold water to remove all of the marinade. Pat dry.
4. Spoon the processed mixture onto the roast a little at a time, coating the meat evenly. Using kitchen twine, close the roast and tie it shut, then coat the outside of the meat with any remaining mixture.
5. In a large, ovenproof sauté pan, heat 2 tablespoons of oil until it shimmers. Place the roast into the pan and brown all over—about 4 minutes per turn. When it is browned all over, transfer the pan to the oven rack with 1½ to 2 cups water in a small pan on the lower rack.

6. When the roast has been cooking for 60 minutes, insert a meat thermometer into the thickest part, then baste the meat with the juices that accumulate in the pan. If the water has evaporated from its pan, carefully add more, and return the roast to the oven and cook until the internal temperature reaches 145°F— about another 20 minutes.
7. When the internal temperature reaches 145°F, remove the roast from the oven, transfer it to a cutting board, and cover with foil for fifteen minutes before carving.

Wilted Spinach Salad with Bacon Dressing

Ingredients:

- 10 to 12 oz. fresh spinach, washed and torn into bit-size pieces
- ¼ cup minced red onion
- 6 radishes, washed and thinly sliced
- 2 hardboiled eggs, peeled and rinsed—1 chopped and 1 sliced crosswise
- 4 slices smoked bacon
- 1½ tbsp. bacon fat
- 1½ tbsp. sugar
- 3 tbsp. apple cider vinegar
- 1 tbsp. water
- ½ tsp. kosher salt
- ⅛ tsp. coarsely ground black pepper

Preparation:

1. Place torn spinach in a large bowl.
2. Add onions and radishes, and refrigerate, tightly covered, for 2 to 3 hours.
3. Fry the bacon in a medium sauté pan until crisp; transfer bacon to a plate covered with a paper towel and reserve the fat.
4. Combine the fat with the sugar, vinegar, water, salt, and pepper in a microwave-safe container and mix thoroughly, then refrigerate until just before serving.
5. When ready to serve, microwave the dressing on high for 30 to 45 seconds, or until mixture boils. Mix the chopped egg into the spinach leaves, then pour the hot dressing over greens mixture and toss lightly.
6. Top with the sliced egg and crumbled bacon and serve.

Nicoise Olive Mashed Potatoes

Ingredients:

- 1 lb. (about 4 medium) Yukon Gold potatoes, cut into 2-inch cubes
- 1½ quarts water
- 2 tbsp. butter
- 1/3 cup Nicoise olives, pitted and minced
- 2 tbsp. sour cream
- kosher salt and black pepper, to taste

Preparation:

1. Place the potatoes into a 4-quart stockpot and boil until tender—about 18 to 20 minutes.
2. Pour the potatoes and water through a colander, then return the potatoes to the pot.
3. Add the butter, olives, and sour cream; and mash thoroughly. Add salt and pepper to taste.
4. Transfer to a bowl and serve with the roast boar leg.

OvenRoasted Garlic Green Beans

Ingredients:

- 3 tbsp. extra-virgin olive oil
- 1 lb. fresh green beans, rinsed and dried, then trimmed to remove stems
- 1 tbsp. granulated garlic

Preparation:

1. Place the olive oil in a flat, shallow dish or pan.
2. Roll the beans in the oil to coat each stalk thoroughly, then sprinkle the garlic evenly over the stalks. Roll the stalks as needed to ensure even coverage.
3. Transfer the stalks to a lightly greased cookie sheet and place it on the lower rack of the oven when the roast boar leg is done. Roast the beans for 15 minutes, then transfer to a serving dish, and serve with the roast boar leg and olive mashed potatoes.

Suggested Accompaniment

- *Cabernet Sauvignon:* Rowland Cellars Cenay—Napa Valley, California, or Chateau St. Michelle—Columbia Valley, Washington

Roast Leg of Wild Boar

Krazy Kingfish

Ocean fishing has been a passion of mine since my dad used to take me to Westport, Washington, to fish for salmon. So when I heard that a variety of pelagic fish could be caught out of Savannah, my excitement level began to rise.

In late June of 2004, Kevin, a friend and work colleague, called one day with an invitation to go off-shore fishing with him and his friend Bill on Bill's twenty-six-foot Grady White fishing boat. He didn't have to ask twice!

In making preparations for the trip, I asked Kevin what we needed to bring, and his reply wasn't what I expected: Bill had everything and didn't want us to bring anything other than our food and drinks!

The day of the trip arrived, and my wife Susan and I picked up Kevin and his wife Mary before dawn and headed toward the Ft. McAllister Marina, a short five-minute drive from our home. Bill greeted us on the main walkway to the docks and after introductions, headed back down the dock.

"What kind of bait do we need?" I asked as we passed a large chest freezer with a "Frozen Bait" sign taped to the top and two large live wells full of shrimp and pinfish.

"I already have everything on board, so let's get going," Bill replied. "We have a ninety-minute ride out to the Navy towers, so let's beat some of the traffic!" He then led us to his beautiful boat, which was outfitted with outriggers, a Loran satellite dish, and four-rod holders set with game fishing rods; and we all climbed on board.

The ride from the marina down the Ogeechee River, through St. Catherine's Sound and out into the Atlantic Ocean, was smooth, and the sun was beginning to lighten the eastern skyline. As we raced east-southeast over the gentle swells, Susan and Kevin spotted some small fish that seemed to be "surfing" our wakes.

"What are those?" Susan asked.

"Flying fish," Bill replied. None of the three of us had ever seen a flying fish, and we were fascinated by the bluish-silver, ten-inch fish as they burst out of the leading edge of the wake and flittered ahead a ways before splashing back down into the water.

After a ninety-minute ride, Bill pointed to a large tower in the distance and told us it was "Navy tower #6," then explained that there were eight towers strung along the coast from just south of Charleston, South Carolina down to Brunswick, Georgia, that the Navy uses for off-shore fighter jet training exercises. The tower was also a great place for us to catch some live bait!

Navy Communications Tower – Photo courtesy of U.S. Navy

The tower was still two miles in the distance when Bill cut power to the outboards, slowing us to an idle, and began to rig our rods with ballyhoo. I watched closely so that I could take care of the rigging while Bill piloted the boat. We quickly had the rigs in the water, and Bill set course at a slow troll toward the tower.

Nothing happened for nearly twenty minutes, and the tower was beginning to loom in front of us when the tip of one of the rods began jerking and line began to peel from the reel. Bill immediately cut the engines so that we could concentrate on playing the fish.

I waved Susan over to the rod as I pulled it out of the pole holder and handed it to her.

"What is it?" she asked, wary at taking on too big a fish right off the bat.

"Probably a kingfish," Bill replied.

The reel sang as the fish raced straight away from the boat, so I carefully tightened the drag on the reel. Susan began trying to take back some of the line the fish had peeled off, but within a few minutes, she urged me to take over. I took the rod, and with suggestions from Bill about how to play the strong and aggressive fish, we soon boated a fifteen-pound kingfish.

Kevin snapped a picture as Bill told us that kingfish usually run in schools and tossed both lures back into the water. We trolled the rest of the way to the Navy tower without any action. As we drifted to within thirty yards or so of the tower, Bill stepped below deck and emerged with two "sabiki" rigs—spinning rods rigged with seven feet of stout monofilament line holding twelve tiny hooks and shiny Mylar strips with a two-ounce weight at the end. Quickly locating a school of cigar minnows, Bill cast one of the rigs to the far side of the school, let it sink, then reeled it in, jigging as he reeled. The minnows attacked the flashing Mylar, hooking themselves in the process, and Bill soon lifted six wriggling minnows into the boat. In twenty minutes, we had over fifty minnows in the live well!

We were soon back under way, this time trolling two lines from the outriggers and two lines from the back of the boat. It didn't take long for a fish to grab one of the bait and head for Spain! It was Kevin's turn, so he pulled the rod from its holder and hung on tightly as the fish peeled out line. As he lifted the rod tip to slow it down a bit, the fish leapt into the air. A mahi-mahi! It gave Kevin a good fight for almost fifteen minutes before he brought it to the boat.

We quickly got the lines back in the water and trolled for several miles around the Navy tower before Bill suggested that we head over to an underwater reef to free-spool live bait for kingfish. He explained that we would rig some wire leaders with live cigar minnows, then let them swim on their own with an open reel. There would be just enough drag to make them appear wounded, and the kingfish wouldn't be able to resist.

A few minutes later, a large fish grabbed my minnow and took off. When I closed the bale on the reel and set the hook, the fish did not appreciate it!

"That's a barracuda!" Bill said, watching the fish thrash below us. Barracuda are great fighters, and this one proved it, alternatively running away from the boat and diving for the depths. When I finally had it alongside, Bill reached over the side of the boat, grabbed it by the tail with a chain-mail glove, and dragged it into the boat. Kevin pinned the thrashing fish to the deck and was able to remove the hook without injuring it. Bill then flipped it back over the side, and it wasted no time streaking away from us.

After sacrificing a dozen more cigar minnows to the marauding barracuda, we decided to start trolling toward home. The sun was sliding toward the western horizon and we still had a sixty-mile run back to the marina, so Kevin and I re-rigged the rods with skirted ballyhoos.

Shortly after beginning our new troll, one of the rod tips jerked toward the water, and we heard the sweet sound of line being ripped from the reel. As I lifted the rod from the holder and handed it to Kevin, one of the other rods jerked wildly, signaling that another fish had taken the bait. Fortunately, we were each able to bring our fish to the boat without any tangles or other incidents.

We continued trolling and caught two more kingfish before noticing several thunderheads building on the western skyline and deciding we'd better get to the marina as quickly as possible. Stowing the rigs, we watched as a nasty little thunder storm built in front of us, and a heavy rain began to fall as we crossed St. Catherine's Sound and entered the mouth of the Ogeechee River. We arrived at the marina soaking wet, but as we emptied the fish hold of those Krazy Kingfish, we agreed that this had been trip to remember.

Smoked King Mackerel Dip

Brining Ingredients:

- One 3-4 lb. boneless kingfish fillet, cut in half
- 1 qt. cold water
- 1 cup brown sugar
- ¼ cup kosher salt
- 3 cloves minced garlic
- 1 tsp. whole black peppercorns
- 2 bay leaves
- ¼ cup soy sauce

Preparation:

1. Mix the water, brown sugar, salt, garlic, peppercorns, bay leaves, and soy sauce in a glass or plastic container. Add the fish and refrigerate for at least 4 hours or overnight.
2. Remove the fish and pat dry.
3. Soak 2 cups of mesquite or hickory wood smoking chips in water for 5 to 10 minutes, then remove and drain.
4. Light a dozen charcoal briquettes in an aluminum pie tin placed inside a Weber or other barbeque. When the coals are covered in a thin layer of white ash, spread them evenly in the tin and lay a handful of the wood chips on the coals.
5. Place the fish on the cooking grate as far from direct heat as possible. Close the barbeque's lid. Add additional wood chips every 30 to 45 minutes.
6. Smoke the fish until it is firm to the touch but avoid allowing the meat to become too dry inside.

Dip Ingredients:

- 3 to 4 lb. of smoked king mackerel, flaked
- 1 cup low-fat mayonnaise
- 1 cup fat-free sour cream
- 1 cup fresh parsley, chopped
- 2 tbsp. yellow mustard
- 1 medium onion, diced
- 2 tbsp. celery salt
- 4 tbsp. Worcestershire sauce
- 4 garlic cloves, minced
- 1 tbsp. coarsely ground black pepper
- 2 tsp. lemon juice
- ½ tsp. horseradish (optional, to taste)

Preparation:

1. Mix all of the ingredients except for the mackerel in a large, nonreactive bowl.
2. Add the mackerel and mix thoroughly. Test taste the mixture, and add any additional seasoning desired.
3. Transfer 1 to 2 cups of the mixture to a serving bowl and serve with sweet gherkin pickles, capers, and stone-ground wheat or water crackers.

Shredded Fennel, Apple, and Asiago Cheese Salad

Ingredients:

- 2 fennel bulbs, halved and sliced thinly lengthwise, fronds removed and reserved
- 2 Granny Smith apples, halved, cored, and cut into thin slices
- ½ cup Asiago cheese, shaved with a vegetable peeler into large "sheets"
- 1 tbsp. lemon zest
- ¼ cup extra-virgin olive oil
- 2 tbsp. fresh basil leaves, coarsely chopped
- Kosher salt and coarsely ground black pepper, to taste

Preparation:

1. Chop 1 tablespoon of the fennel fronds and set aside.
2. Combine the fennel and apple slices in a large mixing bowl. Add the cheese, zest, oil, and basil. Toss gently, then taste and season, if needed, with salt and pepper.
3. Arrange the salad on chilled individual serving plates and top with the chopped fennel fronds.

MahiMahi Cubana

Ingredients:

- 2 lb. mahi-mahi fillets, skin removed
- ½ cup dark rum
- ½ cup fresh lime juice
- 2 onion, cut crosswise into ¼-inch slices
- 1 lemon, cut crosswise into ¼-inch slices
- 2 tsp. dried oregano
- 4 tbsp. butter
- kosher salt and ground black pepper to taste

Preparation:

1. Place the fillets in an ovenproof 9×13 glass baking dish. Pour the rum and lime juice over the fish, and place a sliced onion on each fillet. Cover and refrigerate for 2 to 4 hours.
2. Preheat the oven to 325°F (165°C).
3. Remove fish from the refrigerator and pour off about 3/4 of the liquid.
4. Leave the onion slices on the fish and place a thick slice of lemon over the onion slices fillet. Sprinkle each fillet with oregano, salt, and pepper to taste. Finally, place a pat of butter or margarine on each fillet.
5. Bake, covered, for about 20 to 30 minutes or until fish flakes easily with a fork. Do not overcook the fish or it will be dry. Serve with the cooked onion and lemon slices.

Sauted Mushrooms

Ingredients:

- ¼ cup butter, melted
- 3 garlic cloves, minced
- ¼ cup fresh basil, chopped
- ½ lb. large, fresh shiitake or portabella mushrooms, stems removed and sliced
- grey sea salt and medium-grind white pepper, to taste

Preparation:

1. Combine the butter, garlic, and basil in a medium mixing bowl and blend thoroughly.
2. Add the mushroom slices and toss gently to coat.
3. Heat a 12-inch grill pan over medium heat, then transfer the mushrooms to the pan and cook, occasionally stirring gently until the mushrooms have softened—about 6 minutes.
4. Remove from the heat and transfer to a serving bowl, then sprinkle with salt and pepper to taste. Serve immediately

Suggested Accompaniment

- *Beer:* Ice-Cold Red Hook India Pale Ale
- *Sauvignon Blanc:* Marlborough Estate "Zeal"— New Zealand or Santa Digna (Torres)—Chile

Mahi-Mahi Cubana

Cruisin' in Costa Rica

When our friends Donna and Doug called just after New Year's Day 2005 to invite Susan and me to join them and several other friends—Brian and Jen, Bill, and Mike—on a trip to Costa Rica in late January, we quickly accepted—even though Susan had just had foot surgery.

The plan was to fly to Lisbon, Costa Rica—a half-hour drive from our destination of Tamarindo—on a client's Gulfstream III jet. The client owed Doug for handling a tough legal matter and offered the use of his jet in payment. Unfortunately, shortly before our scheduled departure out of Fort Lauderdale, we had to change plans because the client's pilot was nowhere to be found! Fortunately, Donna was able to book us on a commercial flight later that day.

After fighting through rush-hour traffic, we got to Miami International Airport, navigated our way through security to our departure gate, and discovered that the flight had been delayed and moved to a different gate—at the far end of another concourse. Many antics, interesting conversations with strangers (and at least one security guard), and a quick meal, and we finally boarded the plane and departed for San Jose.

We arrived at 1:00 a.m., and a couple of cabs whisked us to our hotel for a short, but welcome, night's sleep. My bag did not show up with the others, so I hung the clothes I was wearing in the closet to air out as much as possible and slept in a hotel bath robe.

Our flight from San Jose to Tamarindo was scheduled to depart at 8:00 a.m., so we checked out of the hotel and were at the terminal by 7:00 without a minute to spare—only to hear that the pilot hadn't shown up and our flight was delayed until 11:00 a.m.!

At 11:00, we boarded a 1975 Piper Caravan twelve-seater, and Susan and Jen were not thrilled! The flight went fine, even though Doug worried the girls further by asking the pilot if we would have to "strafe" the runway—a dirt strip in a pasture—to scare away the Brahma bull that inhabited the pasture. We didn't, and we were soon on our way to the hotel, where Doug, Donna, Susan, and I shared one of two penthouse suites while Jen and Brian shared the other with Bill.

Mike opted not to share a queen bed with Bill, so he had his own room. The hotel, owned by a friend of Doug's, was part hotel and part condos, and the accommodations—including the bar and kitchen we were allowed to use—were great. When we were finally able to relax over a drink, we watched a spectacular sunset over Tamarindo Bay and the Pacific.

Although the airline had said they would deliver my bag that afternoon, Susan sent me to town for a shirt and shorts. A short time later, I met the gang for some "Big as Your Ass Nachos." We couldn't believe the size of the platters of cheese- and chicken-covered nachos, guacamole, and sour cream!

Early the next morning, Doug, Bill, Brian, and I met up with a skipper with whom we would fish that day. The captain was already "tipsy" at 7:30 in the morning, but the young first mate told us that he would handle the boat most of the time.

We fished hard for several hours without success, but we enjoyed an encounter with a huge pod of "spinner" dolphins—named for their habit of rotating two or three times as they leapt out of the water—that easily covered a square quarter mile or more and held at least five hundred animals!

About 2:00 p.m., the captain informed us that it was time to head back to port, but that we would troll for Wahoo and King Mackerel. We caught a brown jack crevalle and purchased a dozen lobsters from some local divers whose boat we encountered.

At Doug's request, our host had bought a nice chateaubriand; so Doug, Brian, and I set about making dinner of broiled spiny lobster, chateaubriand, baked potatoes, and lots of champagne. We went to bed later that night without a complaint in the world!

Two days later, Doug, Donna, and I headed out for half day of fishing. Because we only had a half day to fish, the skipper, Juan, suggested that we stay fairly close to shore and fish for blackfin tuna and Dorado.

Not far off shore, Juan pointed at a school of baitfish leaping out of the water ahead with several four- to six-pound blackfin tuna following inches behind. Juan swung the boat toward the chaos, but we didn't get any strikes after two passes.

Without a word, Doug dug into his large tackle box and pawed through a tray of multicolored lures and handed the first mate, Pedro, a large lure with two treble hooks and a diving blade on its front end. Pedro had never seen anything like it, but he quickly had it in the water.

Zzzzzzz! A fish grabbed the lure and peeled line off the reel. The small lure, diving rather than skipping on the surface, had done the trick. Doug set the hook and handed the rod to Donna, who squealed, "What do I do? What do I do?"

Doug coached her, and she soon had the fish to the boat where Pedro gaffed it. He removed the hooks from the wiggling five-pound fish and shoved it, head first, into a bucket half filled with water.

Doug and Pedro quickly rigged the two other lines with similar lures, and within minutes, we hooked two more fish. Doug and I brought them to the boat quickly, and within fifteen minutes, we had five fat, healthy tuna in the bucket. But as suddenly as it had started, the bite ended.

By this time, the morning sun had climbed well into the sky and was beating down on us. Doug plunged his hands into the ice chest and extracted two Imperial beers, tossing one to me, while Pedro filleted the fish and placed them, safely encased in ziplock bags, in the ice.

"Is anyone ready for something to eat?" Pedro asked.

"Sure! What do you have?" Donna responded first.

"How about tuna sashimi with wasabi soy sauce and beer?" he grinned back.

At first, a sashimi brunch didn't sound appetizing, but Pedro expertly sliced a fillet into bite-sized pieces and laid them on a plate, then mixed a dab of wasabi paste with soy sauce in a small bowl. It looked pretty good!

"Dig in!" he smiled as he handed us each another ice-cold beer.

"It doesn't get any better than this!" we all agreed as we savored fresh fish and tangy sauce with Costa Rica's finest brew.

We truly were Cruisin' in Costa Rica!

Fresh Blackfin Tuna Sashimi

Ingredients:

- 1 lb. boneless blackfin tuna fillet
- ¼ cup low-sodium soy sauce
- 1 tsp. wasabi paste

Preparation:

1. Slice the tuna loin with a sharp knife into ¼-inch pieces. Arrange on a small serving platter.
2. In a small bowl, mix the soy sauce and the wasabi paste thoroughly. Add more soy sauce if too hot, or more wasabi paste if not hot enough.
3. Place the bowl on the platter with the tuna and serve.

Warm Goat Cheese and Balsamic Salad

Ingredients:

- ½ cup extra-virgin olive oil
- ½ tbsp. fresh rosemary, finely diced
- ½ tbsp. fresh thyme
- ½ tbsp. fresh oregano, diced
- 1 8-oz. log goat cheese, cut crosswise into ¼-inch discs
- 1 tsp. Dijon mustard
- 3 tbsp. pomegranate-infused balsamic vinegar
- kosher salt and medium-grind white pepper, to taste
- ½ cup unseasoned bread crumbs
- 1 cup Bibb lettuce, torn or cut into bite-sized pieces
- 1 cup fresh watercress, torn or cut into bite-sized pieces
- 1 cup radicchio, torn or cut into bite-sized pieces

Preparation:

1. Combine the oil and herbs in a small mixing bowl.
2. Place the cheese discs on a small cookie sheet or in a small pan and drizzle with the oil-herb mixture; let stand for 30 minutes
3. Preheat the oven to 350°F.
4. Return the oil-herb mixture to the bowl and chill the cheese discs until firm.
5. Add the mustard, vinegar, salt, and pepper to the mixture; and whisk until blended.
6. Remove the cheese discs from the refrigerator and coat with the breadcrumbs and bake for 10 minutes; remove and set aside.
7. Combine the greens in a large bowl and drizzle with the oil-herb mixture, then toss gently. Transfer to individual salad plates and top each serving with cheese discs.

Steamed Spiny Lobster Tails with Drawn Ginger Butter

Ingredients:

- Four 3 to 4 oz. each spiny lobster tails
- 1 cube butter
- 1 tbsp. extra virgin olive oil
- 2 tsp. fresh ginger, grated

Preparation:

1. Fill a saucepan with a steamer basket with water up to the bottom of the steamer basket and bring to a boil.
2. Place the lobster tails into the steamer basket; cover and steam for 8 to 10 minutes.
3. While the lobster tails are steaming, melt the butter over medium-low heat in a small saucepan.
4. When the butter is melted, stir in the olive oil and the ginger. Cook, stirring, until it becomes fragrant—about 2 minutes. Reduce the heat to very low.
5. Transfer the lobster to a cutting board and remove the shells by snipping, lengthwise, up the underside and the top of the shells, with kitchen shears.
6. Transfer the lobsters to 4 individual warm plates and pour the butter mixture into 4 individual serving dishes; serve immediately.

Dilled Asparagus

Ingredients:

- 1 lb. fresh asparagus, woodsy ends removed
- 1 cup rice vinegar
- ¼ cup fresh dill, coarsely chopped
- 3 tbsp. sugar
- 3 cloves garlic, minced
- kosher salt and coarsely ground black pepper, to taste

Preparation:

1. Steam the asparagus until crisp-tender. Remove from the steamer and plunge into a bowl of ice water; remove and drain.
2. In a large mixing bowl, combine the vinegar, dill, sugar, garlic, salt, and pepper; and stir until the sugar dissolves.
3. Place the asparagus into the mixing bowl and toss to coat.
4. Cover and chill for 6 to 8 hours or overnight.
5. Transfer asparagus to a small serving platter and serve with the lobster.

Suggested Accompaniment

- *Beer:* Ice-Cold Pyramid Hefeweizen Ale (with an orange wedge)
- *Chardonnay:* Columbia Crest Grand Estates—Columbia Valley, Washington, or Rodney Strong Chalk Hill—Sonoma Valley, California

Steamed Spiny Lobster Tails with Drawn Ginger Butter

Storm Surge Scallops

Shortly before Labor Day weekend 2008, our friends Doug and Donna invited Susan and me to go scalloping with them at Horseshoe Beach, Florida. Donna had booked a rental house, and Doug would be bringing their fishing boat, so we quickly accepted!

Although we had never scalloped and had no idea what we were getting ourselves into, we were concerned that Hurricane Rita was strengthening in the Caribbean. The storm's track, however, was projected to take it well to the west toward Louisiana or Texas, so we decided not to worry.

We reached the little burg of Crosstown, just up the road from Horseshoe Beach, after a five-hour drive, picked up a few groceries and our three-day Florida State fishing licenses, then had a ten-minute drive to the rental house.

The house was situated on a series of canals that allowed the residents to moor their boats next to their houses, many of which stood on telephone-pole-sized "stilts," with the ground level decked right up to the water's edge and the upper level decked on three sides. That evening after dinner, we all sat on the upper deck visiting—the girls with their chardonnay, Doug and Barry with a beer, and I with a single malt scotch and a cigar.

The next morning, we motored out of the canals into a narrow channel that led to the bay and followed the channel markers out into the gulf. Large waves, the product of the outgoing tide colliding with an incoming breeze made the going extremely difficult, and we all had to hang on tightly as the boat was slapped around.

Once we cleared the long, narrow channel, we headed north toward the scalloping flats. As the boat came up on plane, we zipped across the water, enjoying the sun sparkling off the clear blue-green water.

What Doug hadn't told us was that the water depth across the bay was barely three feet at low tide, so if we crossed a sand bar, we'd be in real trouble. Fortunately, just about the time I realized this, he spotted a school of baitfish and slowed the boat to a crawl while we rigged a couple of rods with gold spoons.

We dropped the spoons overboard and accelerated to a quick troll, with both lures flashing a couple of inches below the surface. After a few minutes with no luck, Doug decided that we'd better get to the scalloping area before the tide began to change. We reeled in the spoons, stowed the rods, and accelerated again; and before long, we reached the coordinates Doug had loaded into his GPS. He brought the nose of the boat into the wind and dropped anchor. There were thirty or more boats within a hundred yards of us, and we could see lots of people in the water near the boats.

Susan and I weren't experienced snorkelers or scuba divers, so Donna showed us how to "faux-snorkel" by lying on buoyant life jackets to stay afloat. She then climbed over the side of the boat into water that was barely knee deep to alleviate our fears about the water being too deep.

It took Susan and me some trial and error, but we were finally able to stay upright on the life vests and, simultaneously, keep from sucking water through our snorkels. Once we were finally able to focus on finding scallops rather than the distractions of staying afloat and breathing, we were able to catch a few scallops and shove them into long mesh "baskets" hooked to our life vests.

Shortly after paddling away from the boat, I saw two scallops on some grass and reached for them, but they jetted backward into the grass.

I called to Doug as he snorkeled by with his mesh net already almost full to ask how the scallops had done that.

"Look carefully and you'll see a reddish-purple membrane on one side of the shell opening," he replied. "That's their movement sensor. You've got to either be really quick or approach them from the other side!"

"Good to know!" I said back.

Scallops – Photo courtesy of Florida Department of Natural Resources

We soon got the hang of it and filled our mesh baskets in short order. The tide had begun to come in, so it gradually became more difficult for us to reach the scallops as the water deepened. We were all happy to find that, between the five of us, we had nearly filled all five five-gallon plastic buckets!

Arriving back at the rental house, we unloaded our gear and put the buckets of scallops into Doug's truck for him to take to a fish market to exchange for some that had already been shelled. When he returned, Doug told us he'd found a local fishing guide for the afternoon, so after scalloping the next morning, we made our way to the guide's place, shook hands, and climbed aboard his boat. The prey that afternoon would be sea trout, redfish, and Spanish mackerel.

Over the next hour, we caught several redfish, keeping one, but didn't catch any trout. With evening fast approaching, the guide rigged us for mackerel.

The setting sun and the changing tide signaled "feeding time" to the mackerel, and we soon had three fish in the boat. Two more circular passes didn't result in any more strikes, so we reeled in and headed for port.

Spanish Mackerel

Back at the house, I offered to fix the redfish for dinner.

"No, thanks," Doug replied. "We're going to drive up to the next town to visit some friends of ours."

"We are?" asked Donna, obviously unaware of Doug's plan.

Twenty minutes later, Susan and I had the place to ourselves. We had a light dinner, enjoyed the evening on the deck, and were sleeping soundly when we were awakened by pounding on the front door.

"It's your neighbor," the voice from the other side of the door shouted. "You need to rescue your gear! The storm surge is almost above the deck!"

Throwing on jeans and T-shirts, Susan and I raced down the stairs to the ground level where the water had reached the top of the dock and was still rising, threatening the gear we had spread across the wooden platform to dry.

We shuttled everything from dockside to a grassy mound next to the house, hoping it would be high enough to stay above water. As we deposited the last of the gear on the mound, Doug, Donna, and Barry pulled in, the truck's headlights shining on Susan and me.

"What's going on?" Donna asked as she climbed out of the truck.

"Storm surge—from the hurricane!" I answered.

By this time, the water level was starting to recede—several inches below the crest of the grassy mound, signaling that the worst had passed.

"Where are Doug and Barry?" Susan asked.

"We'll talk about *that* some other time!" Donna replied, not smiling. Without elaborating, I could say that Doug and Barry slept in the cab of the truck that night.

The next morning, as if nothing had happened, Doug asked, "So how come all of our gear is piled up on the grass?"

Donna said, "Just say, 'Thank you, Susan and Stan!'"

Realizing that the less he said the better, Doug said, "Thank you!"

"You're welcome," I responded, laughing. "Just send us home with a couple of bags of scallops and we'll call it even!"

"You got it!" he quickly agreed, and a short time later, we bid our farewells and headed home with our "Storm Surge Scallops."

Spanish Mackerel Ceviche

Ingredients:

- 2 fresh 6 oz. Spanish mackerel fillets, chilled to 320–34°F, but not frozen
- fresh-squeezed Meyer lemon, lime, and/or Naval orange juice—enough to cover the fish and scallops
- 1 tbsp. white wine vinegar
- 1 tbsp. olive oil
- 1 tsp. kosher salt
- 1 tsp. coarsely ground black pepper
- 2 scallions, sliced
- 1 Roma tomato, seeded and diced
- ¼ cup chopped cilantro
- 4 Bib lettuce leaves, rinsed and dried
- 4 to 6 Mandarin orange segments

Preparation:

1. Cut the fish into strips and place in a nonreactive bowl.
2. Mix together the juice, the vinegar, oil, and seasoning; and then pour over the fish, ensuring that all the strips are covered.
3. Seal the bowl with plastic wrap and refrigerate until the fish's flesh turns opaque.
4. Remove the fish from the marinade and pat dry.
5. Combine the scallions, tomato, and the cilantro with the fish, then spoon onto each lettuce leaf with the orange segments arranged on top.

Braised Fennel, Carrots, and Apples

Ingredients:

- 1 tbsp. olive oil
- 2 cups fennel bulb, washed and cut crosswise into ¼-inch slices
- 2 cups carrots, washed, peeled, and cut into thin 2-inch strips
- 1 cup red onion, washed, peeled, and coarsely chopped
- 2 cups Granny Smith apples, washed, cored, and thinly sliced
- ½ cup apple cider
- ¼ cup apple cider vinegar
- ¼ cup honey
- 2 tbsp. brown mustard
- 2 tbsp. fresh basil, coarsely chopped
- kosher salt and coarsely ground black pepper, to taste

Preparation:

1. Heat the olive oil in a medium sauté pan over medium heat and cook the fennel, carrots, and onion, stirring often, until they begin to caramelize.
2. Add the apple slices, juice, vinegar, honey, and mustard; and stir gently to integrate. Cover and cook for 10 minutes, then uncover and cook until the liquid is absorbed and the vegetables are glazed.
3. Transfer to a serving bowl; sprinkle on the basil, salt, and pepper; and toss gently, then serve.

Seafood Mélange with Tuscan Pesto over Whole Wheat Fettuccini

Pesto Ingredients:

- 3 tbsp. fresh rosemary leaves
- 2 tbsp. fresh parsley leaves
- 1 tbsp. fresh oregano leaves
- 4 fresh sage leaves
- 2 cloves garlic, minced
- ½ tsp. chili powder
- 1 tsp. kosher salt
- 1 tbsp. coarsely ground black pepper
- ¼ cup extra-virgin olive oil

Pesto Preparation:

1. Rinse, dry, and coarsely chop the rosemary, parsley, oregano, and sage leaves
2. Combine all ingredients in a small food processor and puree until thoroughly blended.

Mélange Ingredients:

- 2 qt. water
- 1 tsp. vegetable or olive oil
- ½ tsp. kosher salt
- 1 pound (dry) whole wheat fettuccine pasta
- 1 tbsp. extra-virgin olive oil
- ½ tbsp. butter
- ¼ tsp. cayenne pepper (optional)
- ½ cup red bell pepper, chopped
- ½ lb. bay scallops, washed, rinsed and drained
- ½ lb. fresh shrimp, headed, peeled and deveined
- ½ lb. red drum boneless fillet, cut into 1-inch cubes
- ½ lb. mussels, rinsed, de-bearded, steamed open (and removed from shells, if desired)
- ½ lb. fresh crab meat, picked and rinsed
- 1 cup freshly grated Asiago cheese

Mélange Preparation:

1. Bring the water, oil, and salt to boil in a 4-quart stockpot. Add the fettuccine and boil for 10 minutes.
2. While the pasta water is coming to a boil, heat the olive oil and butter in a large sauté pan over medium heat until the oil shimmers and the foam begins to subside.
3. Add the cayenne, onions, and peppers; and cook, stirring occasionally, until the onions are tender—about 4 minutes. Add the garlic and cook for 2 more minutes.
4. Add the scallops, shrimp, and fish; and cook, stirring, for 2 minutes until everything in the pan is thoroughly mixed together.
5. Add the Tuscan pesto, the mussels, and the crabmeat; and stir gently until the fish flakes apart.
6. Drain the pasta in a colander, then transfer both the pasta and the mélange to a serving bowl and sprinkle with the grated cheese. Serve immediately.

Fresh Fruit Sherbet

Ingredients:

- 2 cups fat-free yogurt
- 1 box sugar-free plain gelatin
- 1 tbsp. vanilla extract
- ½ cup each fresh raspberries and blackberries

Preparation:

1. Combine the yogurt, gelatin, vanilla, and berries in a food processor and process until smooth.
2. Spoon the mixture into individual parfait glasses and chill or freeze until serving time.

Suggested Accompaniment

- *Beer:* Ice-Cold Dos Equis with a lime wedge
- *Pinot Grigio:* Clos Du Bois—Geyserville, California, or Oxford Landing—South Australia

Spanish Mackerel Ceviche

A Late First

The state of Washington did not have a huntable population of wild turkeys until shortly before I moved to Georgia in 1999. So when I learned that they were common in and around the Savannah area, I began to fantasize about the opportunity to hunt them.

Fast-forward to 2009 when I met David, a retired ATF agent married to a woman with whom I worked. David was an avid turkey hunter and was more than willing to teach me whatever he could. He had grown up hunting and fishing in Alabama, becoming something of a turkey-hunting expert, and it was not unusual for him to shoot his three-bird limit in the first day or two of the season!

Fort Stewart, Georgia, just up the road from us, offers an annual civilian hunting and fishing pass, and giving hunters fairly open access to a huge amount of wilderness that harbors turkeys, quail, coyotes, foxes, rabbits, deer, and feral hogs, plus dozens of lakes and ponds that hold plenty of bass, bream, crappie, and catfish. In other words, it was a sportsman's paradise!

Unfortunately, periodic closures of designated hunting areas made it difficult to do much quality scouting—which David considered a "must" for successful turkey hunting—and our 2010 season closed with a couple of close calls but no birds on the ground. Disappointed but not deterred, David's affable personality got him introduced to several members of local hunting "clubs"—collective leases of timber company land—and one of those introductions resulted in both of us becoming members of a club that looked very promising for both turkeys and deer.

A month before the season David, with me in tow, began walking the property, becoming familiar with its clear cuts, newly planted sections, and hardwoods. The hardwoods were our primary focus because they provided plenty of acorns and bugs for the birds as well as fairly open expanses in which they could strut. We found several hardwood "plots" with lots of turkey sign, and David was clearly encouraged.

"Let's see how often they come through here," he said one morning as we came upon a newly scratched area. "I brought some corn for us to spread out, and if they come through regularly, we'll be able to see by the day after tomorrow if they've been here." So working in opposite directions, we flung about five pounds of corn kernels across an area about twenty-five feet square, then continued to another hardwood flat and did the same thing.

Two days later, we confirmed that the birds had found the corn—both woodlots looked like someone had come through with a roto-tiller! Excited, we repeated the process, spreading more corn, and after two more days, concluded that the birds were "cruising" the entire area either every day or every other day.

The weather on opening day of the 2011 season was clear and mild. Whispering in the dim glow of our vehicles' interior lights, we quickly decided that David would hunt the hardwood bottom closest to our vehicles while I would make my way further down the edge of a clear cut before angling into the woods to the edge of a dry swamp.

I found my spot about fifteen minutes before first light and quickly set up a camouflaged burlap ground blind, then positioned three hen turkey decoys about twenty yards in front of the blind. Once situated, I arranged my gear—a slate call, a box call, and my binoculars—so that they were handy but out of the way and laid my twelve-gauge side-by-side shotgun across my lap.

As the decoys began to take shape in the first vestiges of morning light, I made a few light strokes on the box call. Almost instantly, I heard my first-ever gobble far in the distance to my right! Waiting another five minutes as the light increased around me, I stroked the box call again and, again, was answered with another gobble.

Just about that time, as I glanced to my right and left to see if any turkeys had snuck in without me seeing them, I saw two shotgun shells laying a few feet away on top of the log on which I was sitting. "You idiot!" I said to myself as I slowly and quietly opened the breach to my gun and slid the shells into the chambers. Thank goodness I had noticed them before I had a turkey in front of me!

Resettled, I stroked the call again and was answered instantly. This time, though, I could tell that the tom had left his roost and was coming my way! I hunkered down behind the burlap screen, again looking right and left. About twenty minutes had passed since the first gobble, and it was light enough to see any approaching birds.

Suddenly, I heard the *crunch, crunch, crunch* of something coming toward me from my left. As I turned as slowly as possible toward the sounds, the shapes of three turkeys materialized from between the trees and shrubs, and they were all but running toward the decoys! As they came closer, I was able to determine that all three were "jakes"— yearling males—with "beards" about two inches long jutting from the center of their chests.

As the jakes rushed in, I hit the box call again to see if the tom that had been gobbling at me was still coming toward me from the other direction. A loud gobble confirmed that he was—and that he was closing the distance between us very quickly. I would soon have three jakes and a mature tom right in front of me!

It quickly became clear that the jakes might pose a problem: one was standing less than five yards in front of my blind, scanning the area intently. Fortunately, as the gobbler appeared in the distance— at full strut even as he walked toward the blind—the jakes turned their attention to him, and I was able to shift to a shooting position.

Things happened very quickly at that point. The gobbler, seeing the jakes and the hen decoys, bee-lined it straight at me, gobbling a couple of times and pausing to strut once. It was all I could do to avoid staring at his bright blue head, broad fan, and nine-inch "beard!" Almost before I knew it, the gobbler, a hen that had appeared out of nowhere, plus the three jakes, filled my view. They milled around, scratched the ground, and investigated the decoys for a minute or two, then began to leave.

I knew that I had to do something or lose any opportunity. I raised my gun, poking the barrel through a small hole in the blind. By this time, though, the small flock was moving away quickly.

The tom trailed the rest of the group, so I decided that I would take a shot when he cleared the tree. I was a little concerned about the distance—the tree was between forty and forty-five yards away— but was confident in my gun's knockdown capability.

As the large bird stepped from behind the tree, I slowly squeezed the trigger. The gun roared, and I could see the gobbler tumble forward, flapping his black-and-white barred wings. I watched for a few moments as the jakes at first scattered, then came back to see what had happened to their patriarch. I thought for a moment about shooting one of them as they stood over the fallen bird but decided that I should leave them for another hunt.

As I rose from behind the blind, the young birds ran, clucking loudly, into the underbrush. I counted off fifty paces to where the gorgeous bird lay, still flapping occasionally.

The beautiful bird wasn't going anywhere though, and as I knelt beside him, I said a couple of quick "thank you's:" first, to David for all of his diligent preparations and patience with me; and second, to the forest gods for my first wild turkey—even if it was kind of late in my hunting life!

Bacon and Potato Tart

Ingredients:

- 10 slices of thick-cut bacon, cut into ¼-inch pieces
- 1 medium yellow onion, peeled and coarsely chopped
- 1 medium russet potato, peeled and coarsely shredded
- 2 tbsp. champagne vinegar
- 2 tsp. chives, chopped
- 1 tsp. fresh sage, chopped
- kosher salt and coarsely ground black pepper, to taste
- prepared pizza dough, thawed
- ¼ cup crème fraiche
- ⅛ tsp. ground nutmeg

Preparation:

1. Preheat the oven to 500°F.
2. Cook the bacon pieces in a large sauté pan over medium heat until lightly browned. Remove with a slotted spoon to a plate covered with a paper towel.
3. Add the onion to the pan and cook until lightly browned—about 2 minutes— then add the potato and cook, stirring, for another 3 minutes. Add a little water if the potato begins to stick.
4. Stir in the vinegar, chives, and sage, plus a little salt and pepper, then remove from the heat.
5. Roll out the dough on a lightly floured surface into a 9×12-inch rectangle, then transfer it to a lightly floured baking sheet, stretching it back to size if necessary.
6. Combine the crème fraiche and the nutmeg with the onion-potato mixture and stir to blend thoroughly, then spread the mixture over the dough, leaving a border of about ½ inches on all sides.
7. Bake the tart for 12 minutes, then remove to a cutting board, cut into 2-inch squares, and serve hot.

Tossed Salad with Toasted Walnuts, Avocado, and California Dressing

Ingredients:

- ¼ cup sunflower oil
- 2 tbsp. champagne vinegar
- 1 tbsp. sugar
- 2 tsp. dried parsley flakes
- ½ tsp. minced garlic
- ¼ tsp. dry mustard
- ¼ tsp. dried oregano
- ¼ tsp. medium ground white pepper
- 1 head red leaf lettuce, torn or chopped into bite-sized pieces
- ½ cup walnuts, toasted and coarsely chopped
- 1 cup cherry tomatoes, washed halved
- 2 large avocados, peeled, pitted, and cut lengthwise into 8 wedges

Preparation:

1. Preheat the oven to 350°F.
2. Thoroughly mix together the oil, vinegar, sugar, parsley flakes, garlic, dry mustard, oregano, and pepper in a nonreactive container.
3. Spread the walnuts evenly on a cookie sheet and bake for 10 minutes, then transfer them to a cutting board and coarsely chop them.
4. Place the lettuce leaves in a serving bowl, sprinkle in half of the walnuts and tomatoes, then half of the dressing. Toss lightly, then repeat with the rest of the walnuts, tomatoes, and dressing.
5. Garnish with the avocado wedges and serve.

Baby Peas and Shiitake Mushrooms

Ingredients:

- 2 cups (16 oz.) fresh or frozen baby peas
- ½ cup shiitake mushrooms, rinsed and sliced into
- ¼-inch pieces
- ½ cup water
- 1 tbsp. butter

Preparation:

1. In a 1-quart saucepan with a steamer insert, combine the peas and mushrooms, bring the water to a boil, and steam until tender—about 6 minutes.
2. Transfer to a serving bowl, stir in the butter, and serve.

Marinated and SmokeRoasted Wild Turkey

Unlike many hunters, I have always preferred to dress wild birds essentially the same as a domestic bird is dressed—except to skin, rather than pluck, them. Skinning avoids having to deal with the feathers (and even more so, the down that clings to *everything*) and reveals the shot holes so that the pellets can be removed more easily. Many argue that the legs of upland game birds (and turkeys) are tough and stringy, and that there isn't enough meat on the legs of waterfowl to bother with. Regardless of your preference, this recipe will make the most of your wild turkey—breast only, or the whole bird.

Marinade Ingredients:

- 1 cup extra-virgin olive oil
- 2 cups dry white wine
- ½ cup Tarragon vinegar
- 1 tbsp. fresh, coarsely chopped sage leaves (or ½ tbsp. dried chopped sage leaves)
- 1 tbsp. fresh (½ tbsp. dried) thyme
- ½ tbsp. cloves
- 1 tsp. ground allspice
- 2 tbsp. kosher or sea salt
- 1 tbsp. ground white pepper

Preparation:

1. The day before cooking time, combine and thoroughly blend the ingredients in a nonreactive bowl.
2. Rinse the bird and shake the water from it, but do not pat it dry. Place the bird into a kitchen trash bag-sized plastic bag, then pour in the marinade. Use your fingers to make sure that the meat is thoroughly coated with the marinade. Rotate the meat inside the plastic bag every 6 to 8 hours.

Entrée Ingredients:

- Marinated whole wild turkey or turkey breast
- ½ cup chicken soup base or bouillon
- 1 tsp. granulated garlic
- kosher salt and coarsely ground black pepper to taste
- 1 cup cold water
- ¼ cup white flour

Preparation:

1. Pre-heat an electric or propane smoker to 275°F.
2. Remove the bird from the plastic bag and rinse it with cold water. Pat dry, then sprinkle it with the garlic, salt, and black pepper.
3. Pour the bouillon in the bottom pan of the smoker and place the bird, either breast up or on its side, in the pan. Place the pan in the smoker, close the door, and fill the wood chip pan with pre-soaked chips.
4. Every 45 minutes or so, check the wood chip pan to keep it stoked and baste the bird with the bouillon.
5. If the bird is laying on its side, flip it over to its other side after 90 minutes.
6. Remove the bird from the pan to a plate and cover loosely with foil.
7. When the internal temperature registers 155°F on a meat thermometer, remove the bird, in the pan, from the smoker. Transfer the bird to a serving platter and cover loosely with foil.
8. In a jar or small mixing bowl, whisk the cold water and flour together thoroughly.
9. Pour the remaining bouillon and juices into a medium-sized saucepan over medium-high heat. When the liquid begins to boil, stir in more (fresh) bouillon if needed and the water-flour mix, whisking until smooth and starting to thicken. Add more salt and/or pepper to taste if needed. Pour the sauce into a gravy boat or bowl and serve with the meat.

Peppery Cane Syrup and Pecan Glazed Sweet Potatoes

Ingredients:

- 3 sweet potatoes, whole, with skin on
- 1 qt. water (or enough to cover the potatoes)
- 2 tsp. medium-ground white pepper
- 1 tbsp. butter, divided into small pieces
- ¼ cup cane syrup
- ¼ cup coarsely chopped pecans
- 2 tbsp. bourbon

Preparation:

1. In a 2-quart stockpot, boil the potatoes in water until tender—about 15 minutes. Remove the potatoes from the pot and allow them to cool to handling temperature.
2. While the potatoes are cooking, combine the pepper, butter, syrup, pecans, and bourbon in a small mixing bowl.
3. Remove the skin and cut each potato into 1-inch cubes and place in a shallow, microwave-proof serving dish.
4. Pour the mixture over the potatoes and toss gently to coat.
5. Microwave on high for 30 seconds; toss again and serve.

Suggested Accompaniment

- *Johannesburg Riesling:* Chateau St. Michelle— Columbia Valley, Washington
- *Pinot Noir:* Primarius—Pendleton, Oregon, or Lindeman's Bin 99—Australia

Marinated and Smoke-Roasted Wild Turkey*
* Capon substituted

Closing Thoughts

I sincerely hope that you have enjoyed reading the adventures and trying the recipes in this book as much as I enjoyed writing and sharing them with you. As depicted in "I Got My Goat (or It Got Me)," the existence of and access to wild game recipes and menus used to be extremely limited, at best. Even with the exponential growth of the number of people interested in wild-game cooking, really good resources are still relatively hard to find, so I, like a few others— Elaine Clarke and Sil Bruning, Rebecca Grey, and Scott Leysath, to name a few—appreciate the opportunity to share some of the things we've learned with those of you who appreciate the outdoors and its bounties. In doing so, I wanted the approach I chose to make you smile, bring back memories of your own, or inspire you to seek out an adventure you and your loved ones can enjoy together.

Separately, I also hope that you find the recipes and menus contained in these pages interesting, delicious, nutritious, and fun to make and eat. Having evolved from a guy who used to think that over-easy eggs were a major feat to someone who loves to play in the kitchen and create "exotic" dishes, I've tried to offer a few new ideas and ways to cook your game that will help you enjoy the preparation and presentation to your family and guests as much as you'll enjoy eating.

Finally, I hope that you'll let me know what you think of this book—the stories and photos, as well as the recipes and menus. The vast majority of what I know about preparing wild game happened because of help from others, and from old fashioned trial and error, so if I can help you avoid a few of the missteps I've already experienced—and help you avoid any wastage of your wild game—that's a good thing. And if I can learn new things from you, I'm all ears!

So get out and live an outdoor life, then continue your adventures in the kitchen and at the dinner table!

Index

Chardonnay
    14 Hands—Columbia Valley, Washington 196
    Cambria 125
    Chateau St. Michelle "Canoe Ridge" – Columbia Valley, Washington 136
    Columbia Crest Grand Estates—Columbia Valley, Washington 243
    Covey Run—Columbia Valley, Washington 83
    Greg Norman—Australia 83
    Kendall Jackson—Central Coast, California 83
    Rex Goliath—Acampo, California 165
    Rodney Strong "Chalk Hill"—Sonoma Valley, California 243
Chenin Blanc
    Dry Creek Vineyard—Sonoma Valley, California 196
    Graham Beck Game Reserve—South Africa 196
Fume Blanc
    Barnard Griffin—Columbia Valley, Washington 92
    Chateau St. Jean—Sonoma Valley, California 92
Johannesburg Riesling
    Chateau St. Michelle—Columbia Valley, Washington 261
Malbec
    Alamos—Catena Valley, Argentina 110
    Montes—Colchagua Valley, Chile 110
Merlot
    14 Hands—Columbia Valley, Washington 146
    Chateau St. Michelle "Indian Wells"—Columbia Valley, Washington 37
    Concannon Reserve—Livermore Valley, California 146
    Hawkes Vineyard—Sonoma Valley, California 187
    Simi—Sonoma Valley, California 37
Pinot Grigio
    Clos Du Bois—Geyserville, California 252
    King Estate—Willamette Valley, Oregon 65
    Oxford Landing—South Australia 252
    Placido—Tuscany, Italy 65
Pinot Noir
    Bancott—New Zealand 54
    Erath—Eugene, Oregon 54
    Jill's Vineyard—New Zealand 176
    Lindeman's Bin 99—Australia 261
    Primarius—Pendleton, Oregon 261
Pouilly Fuisse
    Lois Jadot—France 46

Riesling
    Covey Run—Columbia Valley, Washington 74
    Penfold's "Thomas Hyland"—South Australia 74
Sauvignon Blanc
    Marlborough Estate "Zeal"—New Zealand 118
    Santa Digna (Torres)—Chile 234
    Snoqualmie Vineyards—Columbia Valley, Washington 46
    William Cole Columbine Reserve—Chile 46
Zinfandel
    Dancing Bull – Modesto, California 102
    James Creek Vineyard—St. Helena, California 102

About the Author

Stan Yockey
Outdoorsman and Chef

An avid outdoorsman, Stan has hunted and fished for fifty-plus years, and is a "life" member of the North American Hunting Club. He has harvested multiple species of big and small game; multiple species of upland birds and waterfowl; many dozens of species of salt water and fresh water fish, plus a variety of shellfish and mollusks; and has prepared an array of appetizers, salads, entrees, and side dishes showcasing his harvests—most using recipes of his own creation. Stan's outdoor pursuits have included forays with his parents, friends, and family, in the Pacific Northwest in his early years, and in the Southeast over the past decade.

While growing up in Seattle, Stan worked in several respected restaurants, including The Golden Lion and The Edgewater Inn, while earning a bachelor's degree in hotel and restaurant management from Washington State University. After graduating, he shifted his business focus, spending twenty years in contract management with The Boeing Company in Seattle, Washington, followed by ten years with Gulfstream Aerospace Corporation in Savannah, Georgia.

Susan, Stan's wife of thirty-six years, consistently supported his outdoor and culinary endeavors, helping and encouraging him to explore new territories—both outdoors and in the kitchen. Embracing this support, Stan penned his first cookbook, *A Life Outdoors (and in the Kitchen!)*, to capture many of his adventures and

provide recipes and menu recommendations based on the game fea
tured in each story. One of these adventures, "Walleye Encounters,"
is featured in the Summer 2012 issue of *Cooking Wild* magazine;
several adventures and menus were later featured in *Richmond Hill
Reflections*—a local magazine in Richmond Hill, Georgia.

Stan currently divides his time between work as a business
management consultant and his continuing pursuit of outdoor and
culinary adventures from his home in Northeast Georgia.